Shedding Silence

Janice Mirikitani

CELESTIALARTS

CELESTIAL ARTS
P.O. Box 7327
Berkeley, California 94707

Cover and Interior Illustrations by Grayce Yamamoto

Cover and text designed by David Charlsen
Typography by Ann Flanagan Typography
Set in Avant Garde and Garamond
Printed and bound at R.R. Donnelley & Sons

Library of Congress Cataloging-in-Publication Data

Mirikitani, Janice.
    Shedding silence.

    I. Title.
PS3563.I696S5   1987   811'.54   86-32715
ISBN 0-89087-496-4
ISBN 0-89087-493-X pbk.

Manufactured in the United States of America

First Printing, 1987

1 2 3 4 5 — 91 90 89 88 87

For Cecil

and four generations of women:

my daughter, Tianne
my mother, Shigemi
and my grandmother, Ichi Inouye

Some of the poems have appeared in:

Amerasia Journal,   (Breaking Silence)
UCLA, (Vol. 8, #2, 1981)

Bamboo Ridge,   (Assaults and Invasions,
Hawaii, Spring 1986   Shadow in Stone)

East Wind Magazine,   (When there is Talk
Summer, 1985   of War)

Practising Angels Anthology, 1986,   (Assaults & Invasions)
Seismograph Press

Breaking Silence, An anthology of   (Breaking Tradition,
Asian American Poets, Greenfield   Breaking Silence)
Review, 1983

Fusion,   (Generations of Women)
San Francisco State Journal,
1983

Hawk's Well, A collection   (Generations of Women)
of Japanese American Art
and Literature, 1986

Contact II,   (It Isn't Easy)
Winter/Spring, 1986

Shedding
Silence

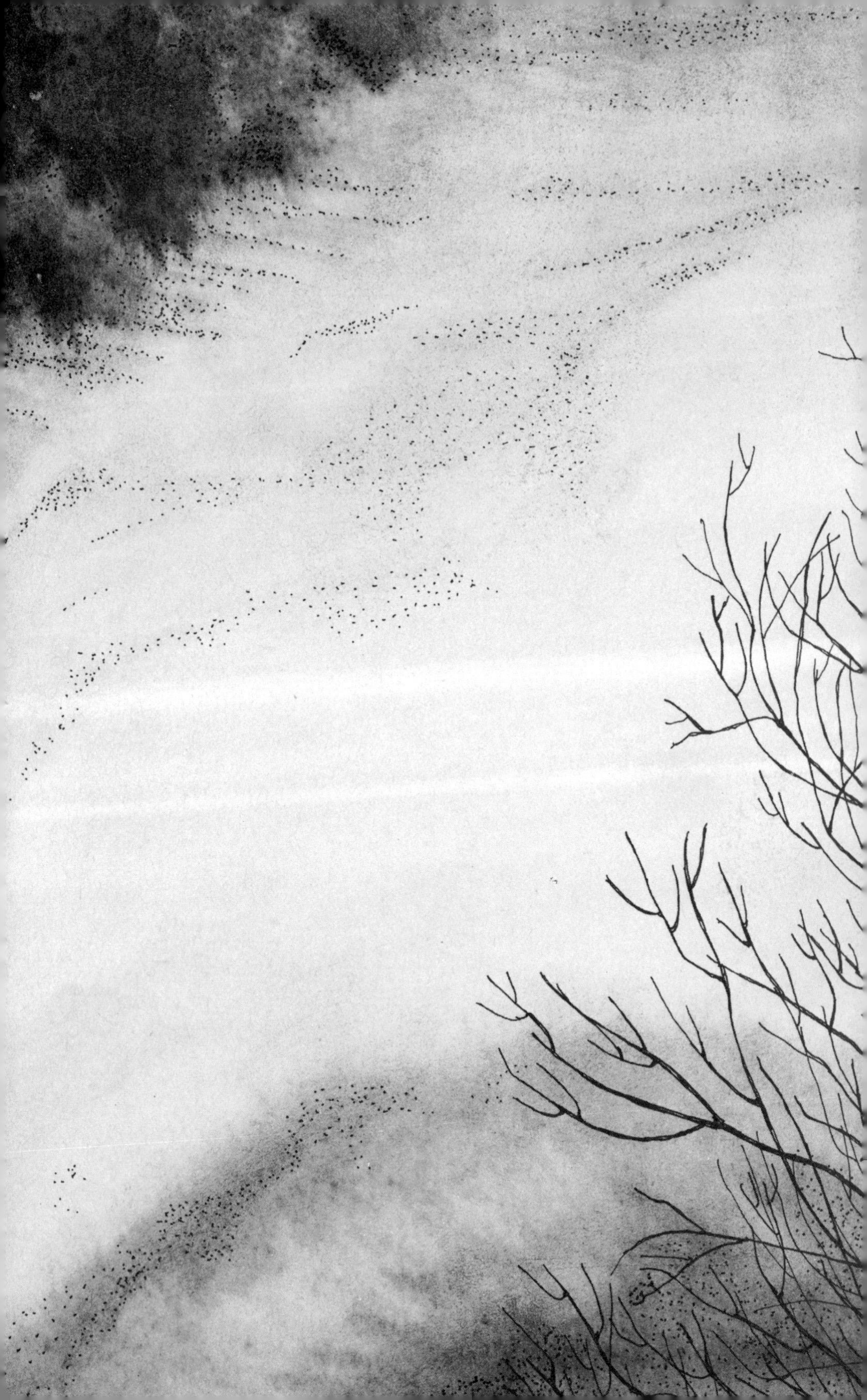

WITHOUT TONGUE

Without Tongue

The sun stood among corn, dead in summer.
Dust whirlwinding off dry fields.
He had awoken her for the last time,
burying his head into her shoulder, clawing
open her thighs like the wide branches of stone pine.
She lay, passive, as always. Breathless. Without tongue,
a dead boat on the bottom of the sea,
a wingless beetle waiting for descending shoe.
She dresses. Walks to the meadow shaded
with hawthorne, oak, white birch.
She lifts the rock where she had buried the knife,
afraid she would use it to kill her father.
Her tongue tastes its cold steel edge,
shrill like blood.
She returns to her kitchen, water steaming
in the kettle. Prepares tea
with leaves of shiso no ha, soaked in kyoto plum
and salt. Dried. Sweet bitterness on her tongue.
Chinese flowers bloom in her throat.
She cleans the blade and returns it to the drawer.

Jade Junkies

They called her Mamasan Kiru.
She could do anything with a knife.
Gut shrimp
with a single slice
dice
an onion before a tear
could slide.
Make cucumber history
each stroke quick
like a blink
thinner than your skin.
Her knuckles
were scarred from so many
knicks.
Some say she was cut deep
when her G.I. split
and left her
in the middle of America.
She couldn't go back home
in disgrace
so she carved out a place,
her one counter cafe
long before sushi
became fashionable
to jade junkies.
She'd dip her fingers
in ginger sauce
leave her scent
in raw bits of flesh
to make them crave

her flavor.
She'd slip fish
from scale to skin
before blood could think
to surface.
Yea, they'd stand in line
to see her magic
with a knife
scale,   skin
   slice
dice,
   chop.

And they'd always ask,
Do you orientals
do everything
so neatly?

Prisons of Silence

(Performed by the Asian American Dance Collective, 1983 Repertory Concert)

1.
The strongest prisons are built
with walls of silence.

2.
Morning light falls between us
like a wall.
We have laid beside each other
as we have for years.
Before the war, when life
would clamor through our windows,
we woke joyfully to the work.

I keep those moments
like a living silent seed.

After day's work, I would
smell the damp soil in his hands,
his hands that felt the outlines
of my body in the velvet
night of summers.

I hold his warm hands to this
cold wall of flesh
as I have for years.

3.
>   Jap!
>   Filthy Jap!
>
>   Who lives within me?
>
>   Abandoned homes, confiscated land,
>   loyalty oaths, barbed wire prisons
>   in a strange wasteland.
>
>   Go home, Jap!
>   Where is home?
>
>   A country of betrayal.
>   No one speaks to us.
>
>   We would not speak to each other.
>
>   We were accused.
>
>   Hands in our hair,
>   hands that spread our legs
>   and searched our thighs for secret weapons,
>   hands that knit barbed wire
>   to cripple our flight.
>
>   Giant hot hands flung me,
>   fluttering, speechless into
>   barbed wire, thorns in a broken wing.
>
>   The strongest prisons are built
>   with walls of silence.

4.
I watched him depart that day
from the tedious wall of wire,
the humps of barracks,
handsome in his uniform.

I would look each day for letters
from a wall of time,
waiting for approach of my deliverance
from a wall of dust.

I do not remember
reading about his death
only the wall of wind
that encased me, as I turned my head.

5.

    U.S. Japs hailed as heroes!

    I do not know the face of this country
    it is inhabited by strangers
    who call me obscene names.

    Jap. Go home.
    Where is home?

    I am alone wandering
    in this desert.

    Where is home?
    Who lives within me?

    A stranger with knife in her tongue
    and broken wing,
    mad from separations and losses cruel
    as hunger.

    Walls suffocate her as a tomb,
    encasing history.

6.
I have kept myself contained
within these walls shaped to my body
and buried my rage.

I rebuilt my life
like a wall, unquestioning.
Obeyed their laws...their laws.

7.

    All persons of Japanese ancestry
        filthy jap.
    Both alien and non-alien
        japs are enemy aliens.
    To be incarcerated
        for their own good
    A military necessity
        The army to handle only the japs.
    Where is home?
    A country of betrayal.

8.
This wall of silence crumbles
from the bigness of their crimes.
This silent wall
crushed by living memory.

He awakens from the tomb
I have made for myself
and unearths my rage.

I must speak.

9.
He faces me in this small
room of myself.
I find the windows
where light escapes.

From this cell of history
this mute grave,
we birth our rage.

We heal our tongues.

We listen to ourselves

    Korematsu, Hirabayashi, Yasui.

We ignite the syllables of our names.

We give testimony.

We hear the bigness of our sounds freed
like many clapping hands,
thundering for reparations.

We give testimony.

Our noise is dangerous.

10.
We beat our hands
like wings healed.

We soar
from these walls of silence.

Generations of Women

I.

    She rests,
rocking to ritual,
the same sun fades
the same blue dress
covering her knees
turned inward
from weariness.
The day is like the work
she shoulders,
sacks of meal, corn, barley.
But her sorrow wears
like steady rain.
She buried him yesterday.
Incense still gathered
in her knuckles knotted
from the rubbings
the massage with nameless
oils, on his swollen gouted feet,
his steel girded back,
muscled from carrying calves,
turning brutal rock,
building fields of promises,
gardens alive with camellias,
peaches, clover.

Time has sucked my body.
He is buried
in his one black suit

we kept in mothballs
for that day.
I want to lay next to him
in my goldthreaded wedding
kimono, grandly purple
with white cranes in flight,
drape my bones with
wisteria.
I want to shed the century
of incense resting in my pores
like sweat or dirt.
I want to fly with the birds
in this eternal silk,
heading sunward
for warm matings.
I want this soil
that wraps him
to sleep in the smell
of my work.

    Obachan
walked to the store
wearing respectable
shoes, leather
hard like a wall
against her sole.
She carefully fingered her coins
in the pocket of her thinning
blue dress,
saved for sugar, salt and yellow onions.
The clerk's single syllable spit
out a white wall—
JAP.
She turned to the door
with shopping bag empty as the sound
of her feet in
respectable shoes.
There are no tears
for moments as these.

II.

Her body speaks,
arms long,
thin as a mantis.

I am afraid
to leave this room
of myself, imprisoned
by walls of cloth.
Only the man clocks
my moments,
as he fingers the
corners of my fabric,
empty buttonholes,
my muslin,
sandy as a desert.
I wait.
I wait for his presence,
my flesh like
sheets drying in the wind.
I wait,
weaving chains of flowers
to scent my hands,
color my skin,
mourn my loss.
I wait
for him to open
the bloom
hidden in the folds
of flannel.
I do not remember
being beautiful or proud.

Some losses
can't be counted:
departures to desert camps
and barracks,
men leaving to separate

camps or wars
and finally to houses
walled white full with women
in silk dresses,
wilted flowers and rhinestones
around their necks,
fast drinking, quick joking
women with red lipstick
sleek
and slippery as satin.
Her thin arms
chained by wringing
and worry
and barbed wire
slashing her youth,
her neck bowed to history
and past pain that haunts
her like a slain woman-child.

> *I watched as they*
> *let her die—seventh sister*
> *born like a blue fish into*
> *that dry orange day.*
> *No more women, they prayed,*
> *a son. A son to carry on the name.*

Some losses can't be counted:
abandonments left her
frightened, hungry,
made her count the grains
of rice,
wrinkles in her cheek,
pieces of rock in the desert
sand, shadows of guardtower
soldiers, mornings without
waking men,
the syllables of her name.
Some imprisonments are permanent:
white walls encaged her

with a single syllable:
JAP.
Her lips puckered
from humiliations
that made her feel like mildewed cloth,
smelling with neglect.
Her body a room
helpless to the exit of men.
The day he left her for the
red-lipped woman,
she, damp, wringing,
stood between desert camps
and bedrooms,
brooding for unburied female infants,
her thin arms dripping chains
of flowers
weighted with tears.

III.

    Two generations
spit me out
like phlegm,
uncooked rice
one syllable words,
a woman foetus.
There are few places
that are mine.
I claim them,
this ground,
this silent piece of sky
where embroidered cranes keep vigil,
this purple silk smelling of mothballs,
this open cage,
this broken wood from Tule Lake.
I keep these like a rock
in my shoe
to remind me not to weep,

to mend my own body,
to wait not for the entry of men
or ghosts.
I claim
my place
in this line of
generations of women,
lean with work,
soft as tea,
open as the tunnels of the sea
driven as the heels of freedom's feet.
Taut fisted with reparations.

Mother, grandmother
speak in me.
I claim their strong fingers
of patience, their knees
bruised with humiliation,
their hurt, longing,
the sinews of their survival.
Generations of yellow women
gather in me
to crush the white wall
not with the wearing of sorrow
not with the mildew of waiting,
not with brooding or bitterness or regret,
not with wilted flowers or red lipstick.
We crush
the white wall
with a word, a glance,
a garden new with nimosa bamboo,
juniper with barbed wire at their root,
splinters from barracks.
We will come like autumn shedding sleep
a sky about to open with rage,
thunder on high rocks.
I crush
the white wall
with my name.

Pronounce it correctly
I say
Curl it on their tongue
Feel each and many
syllable of it,
like grains of warm rice
and that will be pleasing.

Generations of women
spilling each syllable
with a loud, yellow noise.

Doreen

Doreen had a round face.
She tried to change it.
Everybody made fun
of her in school.

Her eyes so narrow
they asked if she could see,
called her moonface and
slits.

Doreen frost tipped her hair
ratted it five inches high,
painted her eyes round,
glittering blue shadow up to her brow.

Made her look sad
even when she smiled.

She cut gym all the time
because the white powder on her neck
and face would streak
when she sweat.

But Doreen had boobs
more than most of us Japanese girls
so she wore tight sweaters
and low cut dresses
even in winter.

She didn't hang
with us,
since she put so much time
into changing her face.

White boys
would snicker when she passed by
and word got around
that Doreen
went all the way,
smoked and drank beer.

She told us
she met a veteran
fresh back from Korea.

Fresh back
his leg
still puckered pink
from landmines.

She told us
it was a kick
to listen to his stories
about how they'd torture
the gooks
hang them from trees
by their feet
grenades
in their crotch
and watch
them sweat.

I asked her
why she didn't dig brothers.

And her eyes
would disappear

laughing
so loud
she couldn't hear herself.

One day,
Doreen riding fast
with her friend
went through the windshield
and tore off
her skin
from scalp to chin.

And we were sad.

Because
no one could remember
Doreen's face.

Recipe

Round Eyes

Ingredients: scissors, Scotch magic transparent tape,
              eyeliner—water based, black.
              Optional: false eyelashes.

Cleanse face thoroughly.

For best results, powder entire face, including eyelids.
    (lighter shades suited to total effect desired)

With scissors, cut magic tape 1/16" wide, 3/4"–1/2" long—
depending on length of eyelid.

Stick firmly onto mid-upper eyelid area
    (looking down into handmirror facilitates finding
    adequate surface)

If using false eyelashes, affix first on lid, folding any
excess lid over the base of eyelash with glue.

Paint black eyeliner on tape and entire lid.

Do not cry.

American Geisha

1.

There are people
who admire
the aesthetics
of our traditions.

And ask politely,
Where are you from?

Lodi
Minneapolis
Chicago
Gilroy
South Bend
Tule Lake
San Francisco
New York
L.A.

They persist and
ask again.

Compliment
our command of the
English language.

2.

American white actress
plays the role
of white American Geisha

filmed on location
in Japan.

It was sooooo hard
says she
because American women walk

in strides

shaking it baby.

Over there,
no hips, no shaking,
point the toes inward and...
don't speak
unless spoken to.

Japanese women,
says she,
don't walk.

They place themselves
like art objects.

3.

Mr. Wong
went to Washington, D.C.
served on a Commission
for Small Businesses.

Was asked
if he was familiar
with the system of free enterprise?

and how come
he didn't speak
with an accent?

4.

They saw
I was Asian
and offered
to revise the program.

So I could read
my poetry
first.

I wouldn't want to follow
HIM.

He is very articulate.

5.

My daughter
was called
F.O.B.

at the beach

bosomed in her swimsuit.

Shake it baby, does it slide sideways?

6.

Do we say thank you?

when they tell us that they've
visited Japan
Hong Kong
Peking
Bali
Guam
Manila
several times

and it's so quaint
lovely
polite
exotic
hospitable
interesting

And when did we arrive?

Since we speak
English so well.

...An Asian American college student was reported to have jumped to her death from her dormitory window. Her body was found two days later under a deep cover of snow. Her suicide note contained an apology to her parents for having received less than a perfect four point grade average...

Suicide Note

How many notes written...
  ink smeared like birdprints in snow.

    not good enough not pretty enough not smart enough
dear mother and father.
I apologize
for disappointing you.
I've worked very hard,
          not good enough
harder, perhaps to please you.
If only I were a son, shoulders broad
as the sunset threading through pine,
I would see the light in my mother's
eyes, or the golden pride reflected
in my father's dream
of my wide, male hands worthy of work
and comfort.
I would swagger through life
muscled and bold and assured,
drawing praises to me
like currents in the bed of wind, virile
with confidence.
    not good enough not strong enough not good enough

I apologize.
Tasks do not come easily.
Each failure, a glacier.
Each disapproval, a bootprint.

Each disappointment,
ice above my river.
So I have worked hard.

                    not good enough

My sacrifice I will drop
bone by bone, perched
on the ledge of my womanhood,
fragile as wings.

                    not strong enough

It is snowing steadily
surely not good weather
for flying—this sparrow
sillied and dizzied by the wind
on the edge.

                    not smart enough

I make this ledge my altar
to offer penance.
This air will not hold me,
the snow burdens my crippled wings,
my tears drop like bitter cloth
softly into the gutter below.

        not good enough not strong enough not smart enough

                    Choices thin as shaved
                    ice. Notes shredded
                    drift like snow

on my broken body,
covers me like whispers
of sorries
sorries.
Perhaps when they find me
they will bury
my bird bones beneath
a sturdy pine
and scatter my feathers like
unspoken song
over this white and cold and silent
breast of earth.

Breaking Tradition

For my daughter

My daughter denies she is like me,
her secretive eyes avoid mine.
    She reveals the hatreds of womanhood
    already veiled behind music and smoke and telephones.
I want to tell her about the empty room
    of myself.
    This room we lock ourselves in
    where whispers live like fungus,
    giggles about small breasts and cellulite,
    where we confine ourselves to jealousies,
    bedridden by menstruation.
    This waiting room where we feel our hands
    are useless, dead speechless clamps
    that need hospitals and forceps and kitchens
    and plugs and ironing boards to make them useful.
I deny I am like my mother.   I remember why:
    She kept her room neat with silence,
    defiance smothered in requirements to be otonashii,
    passion and loudness wrapped in an obi,
    her steps confined to ceremony,
    the weight of her sacrifice she carried like
    a foetus. Guilt passed on in our bones.
I want to break tradition—unlock this room
    where women dress in the dark.
    Discover the lies my mother told me.
    The lies that we are small and powerless
    that our possibilities must be compressed

to the size of pearls, displayed only as
passive chokers, charms around our neck.
Break Tradition.
I want to tell my daughter of this room
of myself
filled with tears of shakuhachi,
the light in my hands,
poems about madness,
the music of yellow guitars,
sounds shaken from barbed wire and
goodbyes and miracles of survival.

My daughter denies she is like me
her secretive eyes are walls of smoke
and music and telephones.
her pouting ruby lips, her skirts
swaying to salsa, Madonna and the Stones.
her thighs displayed in carnavals of color.
I do not know the contents of her room.
She mirrors my aging.

She is breaking tradition.

Shadow in Stone

Journey to Hiroshima, Japan
International Peace Conference, 1984

We wander in the stifling heat
of August.
Hiroshima,
your museum, peace park,
paper cranes rustling whispers
of hei-wa   *peace*
Burning incense
throbbing with white chrysanthemums,
plum blossoms, mounds
of soundless bones.
Hiroshima
how you rise up
in relentless waves of heat.
I come to you late,
when the weather bludgeons, blisters.
          I put my mouth
on your burning sky
on the lips of your murmuring river.
Motoyasu, river of the dead.

          The river speaks:
               I received the bodies
               leaping into my wet arms
               their flesh in flame, and the flies
               that followed
               maggots in the bloated sightless waste,

29

skin rotting like wet leaves.
My rhythm stifled, my movement stilled.

Motoyasu cries with rituals,
bearing a thousand flickering candles
in floating lanterns of yellow, red, blue
to remember the suffering.
I light a lantern for grandmother's sister
whom they never found amidst the ashes
of your cremation.
She floats beside the other souls
as we gather, filling water
in the cups of our hands,
pouring it back into the thirsty mouths
of ghosts, stretching parched throats.

The heat presses like many hands.
I seek solace in the stone
with human shadow burned into its face.
        I want to put my mouth to it
to the shoulders of that body,
my tongue to wet its dusty heart.

        I ask the stone to speak:
                When I looked up,
                I did not see the sun
                a kind friend who has gently pulled
                my rice plants skyward.
                I worried in that moment
                if my child would find shade
                in this unbearable heat
                that melts my eyes.
                No, I did not see the sun.
                I saw what today
                mankind has created
                and I layed my body
                into this cool stone,
                my merciful resting place.

Museum of ruins.
The heat wrings our bodies
with its many fingers.
Photographs remind us of a holocaust
and imagination stumbles, beaten, aghast.
        I want to put my mouth
against these ruins, the distorted teacup,
crippled iron,
melted coins,
a disfigured bowl.

            I ask the bowl to speak:
                The old man
                held his daughter,
                rocking her in his lap,
                day after day after
                that terrible day,
                she weak from radiation
                could not lift this bowl.
                Her face once bright like our sunset
                now white as ash,
                could not part her lips
                as he tried to spoon okayu from this bowl
                droplet by droplet
                into the crack of her mouth,
                the watered rice with umeboshi
                which he would chew to feed her.
                He did not know
                when she stopped breathing
                as he put his mouth to hers
                gently to pass food.
                He rocked her still body
                watching the red sunset
                burning its fiery farewell.

Hiroshima, rising up.
I come here late
when the weather sucks at us.

I want to put my mouth
to the air, its many fingers of heat,
lick the twisted lips
of a disfigured bowl,
the burned and dusty heart of shadow in stone,
put my mouth to the tongues
of a river,
its rhythms, its living water
weeping on the sides of lanterns,
each floating flame, a flickering
voice murmuring
over and over
as I put my mouth
to echo
over and over
never again.

After forty years of silence
about the experience of Japanese
Americans in World War II concentration
camps, my mother testified before the
Commission on Wartime Relocation and
Internment of Japanese American
Civilians in 1981.

Breaking Silence

For my mother

There are miracles that happen
she said.
From the silences
in the glass caves of our ears,
from the crippled tongue,
from the mute, wet eyelash,
testimonies waiting like winter.
    We were told
that silence was better
golden like our skin,
    useful like
go quietly,
    easier like
don't make waves,
    expedient like
horsestalls and deserts.

      "Mr. Commissioner...
      ...the U.S. Army Signal Corps confiscated
      our property...it was subjected to
      vandalism and ravage. All improvements
      we had made before our incarceration
      was stolen or destroyed...

I was coerced into signing documents
giving you authority to take..."
to take
to take.

My mother,
soft as tallow,
words peeling from her
like slivers of yellow flame.
Her testimony,
a vat of boiling water
surging through the coldest
bluest vein.
        She had come to her land
as shovel, hoe and sickle searing
reed and rock and dead brush,
labored to sinew the ground
to soften gardens pregnant with seed
awaiting each silent morning
birthing
fields of flowers,
mustard greens and tomatoes
throbbing like the sea.
        And then
All was hushed for announcements:
        "Take only what you can carry..."
We were made to believe our faces
betrayed us.
Our bodies were loud
with yellow screaming flesh
needing to be silenced
behind barbed wire.

"Mr. Commissioner...
...it seems we were singled out
from others who were under suspicion.
Our neighbors were of German and
Italian descent, some of whom were

not citizens...It seems we were
singled out..."

She had worn her work
like lemon leaves,
shining in her sweat,
driven by her dreams that honed
the blade of her plow.
The land she built
like hope
grew quietly
irises, roses, sweet peas
opening, opening.
      And then
all was hushed for announcements:
      "...to be incarcerated for your own good"
The sounds of her work
bolted in barracks...
silenced.

Mr. Commissioner...
So when you tell me I must limit
testimony,
when you tell me my time is up,
I tell you this:
Pride has kept my lips
pinned by nails
my rage coffined.
But I exhume my past
to claim this time.
My youth is buried in Rohwer,
Obachan's ghost visits Amache Gate.
My niece haunts Tule Lake.
Words are better than tears,
so I spill them.
I kill this,
the silence...

There are miracles that happen
she said,
and everything is made visible.

We see the cracks and fissures in our soil:
We speak of suicides and intimacies,
of longings lush like wet furrows,
of oceans bearing us toward imagined riches,
of burning humiliations and
crimes by the government.
Of self hate and of love that breaks
through silences.

We are lightning and justice.

Our souls become transparent like glass
revealing tears for war-dead sons
red ashes of Hiroshima
jagged wounds from barbed wire.

We must recognize ourselves at last.

We are a rainforest of color
and noise.

We hear everything.

We are unafraid.

Our language is beautiful.

*(Quoted excerpts from my mother's testimony, modified
with her permission)*

Tomatoes

"We have to read The Red Badge of Courage"
"We all had to read it."
"But all heroes are not men."
                              Dialogue with my daughter

Hanako loved her garden. She and her young daughter lived with her parents on a farm planted in the stretch of fields near Gilroy. Her husband died during the war. He was a hero. Received medals and letters of commendation for valor in battle, for defending his country, for saving fellow soldiers in his regiment.

Hanako had delivered to her an American flag and his medal after she and her parents got out of the concentration camp located in the middle of the desert.

When they returned to her parent's farm, the house had to be repaired and rebuilt and the land was dried, cracked like weathered skin.

Hanako would look out over the wide flat expanse of the valley. In the dry season it reminded her of the camp desert where the heat would shimmer up and if you looked long enough you thought you could see someone approaching. She'd do that a lot, dreaming her husband would be running toward her. She'd shade her eyes and watch as the sun pulsated, conjuring up the man with the strong warm hands that would go up her neck and through her hair and pull her face close to him. The heat from the ground would travel through her body and she would weep from the barrenness of knowing he would never be coming back.

Lisa looked like him, his squarish jaw, his deep black eyes, the smile lines in her cheek.

Mommy, I want red flowers.

Hanako set about to soften her earth, make her garden.

She wielded her hoe like a sword, breaking hard crusts of dirt. Lisa would bring out the hose and buckets to help moisten the ground, playing in the water, muddy pools created by Hanako's shovel. She planted bright geraniums that grew sturdily in dry climate next to her tomato vines.

The Haufmanns who lived four acres away came over the day they returned to the farm, talked about the hard times they had during the war and difficulties in keeping up their own land. They just couldn't afford to water anyone else's crops even with the extra money and the furniture, china, tractor, seedlings, livestock they were given by Hanako's parents before their hasty departure to the camps. Mr. Haufmann kicked the dirt as he commented that Hanako didn't look any the worse for wear. He eyed her breasts under her white cotton blouse, and admired how Lisa had grown into a fine young girl with slender hips like her mommy and so sorry
to hear about the husband.

Hanako answered politely
the war is over and done.
We've come back to start our life again
like planting new seeds and hoping they'll
grow stronger.

Mr. Haufmann would frequently visit if he'd see Hanako and Lisa in their resurrected garden, weeding, pulling the dandelion from her tender tomato vines, her sweet peas with their thin delicate stalks climbing the stakes she had hammered into the ground in neat rows, the robust thick stubs of kale, and Lisa's geraniums brightly red in the heat.

Kinda delicate, aren't you, doing
all this work? Skin's going to shrivel
in this mean sun. Work's too heavy for little girls.

Hanako would stand up straight and speak politely, softly,
there are many things we must learn
to do without
and find the strength
to do ourselves.

Lisa, tending her flowers, ran up to Mr. Haufmann who lifted her high in the air, her skirt flying above her panties. Mr. Haufmann laughing, flinging her up again and again, until

Hanako would tell Lisa to finish her watering chores, her eyes turning black and silent as she whacked at the heads of dandelion weeds with her hoe.

The heat rose early that day, its fingers clutching the rows of dirt. Hanako from the kitchen window did not see Lisa in the garden, watering as she usually did. She went immediately outside, looking, instinctively picked up her hoe and walked through the shimmering heat.

Hanako started toward the Haufmann farm when she saw Lisa running toward her with a paper bag.

> Mommy. Mommy. Mr. Haufmann
> gave me pears and figs. They're ripe
> and sweet. He let me climb and pick
> them myself. He's so strong, let me
> stand on his shoulders so I could reach
> the top branches.

Hanako's knuckles turned white on the handle of the hoe, told Lisa she was not to play at the Haufmann's again, returned to her garden and sprayed for insects.

Mr. Haufmann appeared in the waves of heat that afternoon, wiping off his face with the back of his hand. Hanako's sweat ran down her back, popped above her mouth. Haufmann redfaced, smiling

> Tomatoes looking good and juicy.
> Got a lotta nice young buds gonna pop soon, too.
> Heat's good for them I guess.

Hanako with her hoe turned the soil gently,

> How's your wife? Haven't seen her for awhile.

Wetting his lips

> O, that old mare's too tired to
> walk even this distance. Just sits at the
> radio and knits. Damn knitting gets on
> my nerves.

Hanako's hoe, turning, turning

> And your sons. Are they doing well?

Haufmann's hard laugh

> Too good for farming. Both in college,
> and don't hardly write or call. Busy
> chasing women and getting into trouble.
> Ha. Rascals they are. Men will be men.

Hanako's hoe fiercely cutting near the tomato vines

> You are fortunate to have healthy children.

Hanako's hoe high in the air, whacked like a
sword through a ripe tomato, juices springing up, smearing
the soil

>There's nothing we won't do
>to insure their happiness, is there?

her voice low and glinting now like her blade as she whacked
off the head of another tomato smearing the handle red.
Haufmann's eyes, fading lights of blue, blinked as he stepped
backward. Hanako's voice now like the edge of sharp knives
almost whispering

>We see so much of ourselves
>mirrored in our children
>except more...

Whack. Hanako's hoe now fiercely slicing, thudding, crush-
ing the ripened crop of tomatoes as the blade smeared red,
the handle now slippery with juices and pink seeds

>I have no bitterness Mr. Haufmann
>not about the war, nor the losses.

She thought of her husband's final moments.
Did he suffer long. What were his thoughts...

>the humiliation of those camps.

Did he remember her and their chubby Lisa waving
from the wire fence as he left them for the war?

>the work or this heat
>or the loneliness.
>Only the regret
>that my husband

The memory of smile lines in his cheek,
his warm hands stroking Lisa's hair,
quieting her in his rocking arms.

>cannot see the growing,
>budding living hope

Lisa came running to her mother's side, speechless at the
devastation, the red mass of crushed tomatoes, her eyes wide
and instantly older, seeing Haufmann wilting
shriveled in sweat and the wrinkles
of his wet shirt.
He, wordless, slumped
to escape
into the waves of heat.

>Mother. I'm so glad
>you saved my geraniums.

I have seen you

when the delta floods,
packing mud,
sandbags, protecting
the fields like your woman.

in the trees
when the oranges
were ripe,
filling your hands

in strawberry patches
warming buds
against the frost
with your breath.

in a slow dance
eyes closed
remembering the tall grasses
near your village
whispering your name.

I have seen your sons

eyes flaring
in halls of injustice,

commission rooms
spewing yellow rage.

in the lot on Kearny
that yawns like a grave,
kicking the remains
he tried to save.

with shaking hands,
too gentle for words
on the shoulders
of our grandmothers.

I have seen you

    scooping rice and cha
    steamed fish, pansit,
    snow peas and pak-kai
    tsukemono
    into your laughing mouth.

My brothers,
I have seen you.

My eyes blur
sometimes

at beauty.

Slaying Dragon Ladies

On seeing the movie
"The Year of the Dragon"

My fingernails
are long, steel tipped,
sharp as stilettos
to more easily pluck
your eyes,
cleanly sever it from its nerve,
roll it in my palm.
We believe the eye
brings luck, health.
Seasoned with shoyu,
sucked like embryos from eggs.
Ahhh. the nourishment.
My epicanthic fold
lined in red
is the sister of the tiger.
My tongue will moisten
you for easier
swallowing.
Eat your eyes
while I ride you,
my cunt a moving mouth.
Female dragons are born there.
  You don't know me.
  Madame Nhu,
  Anna Chenault,
  Imelda Marcos are not reputed
  for their compassion, after all.

Or you may prefer
my smell to be lush
as damp forests,
exotic as flowered trees.
I dwell in a house of bamboo,
kneeling to the sound of reed flute.
My small hands
folded obediently in my lap.
I wait to serve you
tea,
shuffle to you in
plum scented kimono
on my knees,
speak in whispers
when spoken to and bow
to your growing
fantasy.
      You don't know me.
      Geisha girl.
      China Doll.
      Slant cunt whore.
      Objects dangled
      in the glare.

The sun meets a place
in the sky
and there are no shadows.
You cannot see me.
      my breasts are Manzanar's desert
      my thighs an Arkansas swamp
      my veins are California's railroads
      my feet a Chicago postwar ghetto.
I prepare slowly
with the memory
of my mother who is
civilized,
my father who
fought a war for you,

my grandmother, compassionate,
who forgave you.
My hands are steady.
Pentipped fingers
drenched in ink.
Ready for the slaying.

You will know me.

IT ISN'T EASY

It Isn't Easy

For Cecil

I want to give you
everything
yet nothing...
    my silence
a cup of tea,
chatter...
    the ants
invading our cannisters,
dishes piled like angry words,
dust gathering in corners
like unswept thought...
    It would be easier
this smallness of giving,
this reduction to detail
of maintenance:
the attention to
stockings that need mending,
the filling up of holes,
the knitting of emptiness.
    It would be easier
to be your victim.
Seduced by complacency
effortless acquiescence.
Let you pilot my passive
body into unknown ports...
abdicate to the whirling air
of your arms, and unresisting,

be tossed into the haunches of midnight.
   I want to give you
nothing,
yet everything:
the dreams I navigate
lapping on the shores of
Honshu to the Ivory Coast,
the hibiscus blooming
between my thighs,
   my poems
strung like bloody beads across my throat,
my disembowelment, my seppuku—
scarlet entrails
twisting from the open wound,
   my dark words
unbridled like horses
steaming nostrils, hoof, mane.

   It isn't easy
to bring to your hands
a storm of bloodred flowers
and brutal birthings,
   not easy
this passion for power, my unbeautiful hunger,
this selfish desire to be loud, bigger
than light, this longing
for movement, my own,
this discovery of unveiled women
rising up,
and tongueless ones
rising up...
   this rising up
through empty sockholes,
teacups, dishes, antfilled cannisters,
dust and acquiescence.

It isn't easy
this love rising up
beside your great expanse.
Each lifting its own air,
yellow
dark
feathered flight,
filling the sky
with color and strange song.
A dazzle of independence.

It isn't easy.

In Remembrance

For Uncle Minoru, Died January, 1984

We gather at your coffin,
Uncle Minoru.
Mother, with her hands like gardenias
touches your sleeves.
We whisper of how well you look
peaceful in your utter silence.
How much we remember.
Why now, at death?
      Your kindnesses, Uncle,
as you crafted paper monkeys,
multicolored birds
to climb and jerk on a stick
to amuse children who gathered
at your innocent dark eyes,
always slightly moist.
We would jump on your back, riding you
like a silent horse,
as you lumbered on your hands and knees
from room to room.
      How much we remember...
we rode your shoulders,
knotted with hurt,
dressed in faded denim, smelling like
laundry soap and fish.
You never complained of it
only through those dark moist eyes.
And your smile

52

that drew living animals to you,
even wild birds.
Obachan said they could smell
the wounds hiding in your throat,
the wound in your heart
pierced by unjust punishment, racism, and rejection
sharp as blades.
     When did you vow silence, Minoru?
After the camps,
after you buried a daughter?
You slumped into a light
of your own and let life ride you.
Your daughter thrown broken
on the road by a drunk driver
who mumbled she flew from nowhere like a dumb chicken,
stretched out $200, not one apology
and said we were safer in the camps.
     Was there nothing left to say, Minoru,
as you slapped away his hot white hand?
     How much we remember...
When they took you to Amache Gate
locked us up like herded horses,
your dark innocent eyes, moist
with disbelief at charges of
sabotage, espionage,
your shoulders staggered from the lies.
Fear like a cold finger
pressed at your heart.
Life gasped like a beached fish.
The sky scummed over with clouds
and punishment without crime
stabbed between the blades of your back.
     Was there nothing left to say?
Minoru, the children who rode you
have tongues like birds.
We chatter. We remember
the mounds of hurt at your shoulders.
Could we but massage them to soothe
the pain, but death

makes our regrets scattered as apologies.
We did not expect them
to rip the coat of pride from your bones
nor the melody from your throat.
      Yes, there is much to say.
We will not leave your memory
as a silent rancid rose.
Our tongues become livid with history and
demands for reparations.
Crimes are revealed like the bloody lashes
of a fallen whip:
      the falsehoods, deletions, the conspiracy
      to legalize mass imprisonment.
No, we will not forget
      Amache Gate, Rohwer, Poston, Heart Mountain,
      Minidoka, Jerome, Gila River, Manzanar,
      Topaz, Tule Lake.
Our tongues are sharp like blades,
we overturn furrows of secrecy.
      Yes, we will harvest justice.
And Uncle, perhaps
your spirit will return
alive in a horse, or a bird,
riding free in the wind,
life surging through
the sinews of your strong shoulders.
      And yes,
the struggle continues on
with our stampede of voices.

Soul Food

For Cecil

We prepare
the meal together.
I complain,
hurt, reduced to fury
again by their
subtle insults
insinuations
because I am married to you.
Impossible autonomy, no mind
of my own.

You like your fish
crisp, coated with cornmeal,
fried deep,
sliced mangos to sweeten
the tang of lemons.
My fish is raw,
on shredded lettuce,
lemon slices thin as skin,
wasabe burning like green fire.
You bake the cornbread flat
and dip it in
the thick soup
I've brewed from
turkey carcass, rice gruel,
sesame oil and chervil.

We laugh over watermelon
and bubbling cobbler.

You say,
there are few men
who can stand
to have a woman equal,
upright.

This meal,
unsurpassed.

Spoils of War

Violet ran up the familiar path of **Telman Park** deter-
mined today to make five miles. She knew the exact spot of
her destination, through the eucalyptus, past the emergency
telephone box, up to the twin boulders where she would sit
triumphantly and rest in the warm sun.

He watched her from his green volkswagen van. Her
black hair bouncing at her shoulder blades, her sturdy thighs
and sleek runner's calves. Her small breasts jousled with
each step under the sweatshirt that read, "Lotus Blossom
Doesn't Live Here".

Spirit of the bayonet.
red/harch
white/hup
blue/eyes front
square your piece
left/right
kill 'em
thrust/jab
jab
jab/kill 'em.
"hey mamasan,
joto mate ichiban"
poontang one/two
poontang three/four
when we're done
we'll kill some more.

Of all the joggers he saw, this was the one he wanted.
He would park and watch the several who, at the same time
each day, would run the path up into the wooded hills of
the park.

57

Violet started running after she had met Josh. In fact, she started doing a lot of things. All her life she had been introverted, studious, conscientious, shy. During her last graduate year, life revolted around her. There were so many demonstrations on campus against the Vietnam war, she didn't pay attention to the noises—the speeches, doomsday messages from wild-eyed street preachers and twitching panhandlers. So when the police stormed the gathered protestors, Violet did not move out of the way in time as the sweep of billyclubs and helmets picked her up like a wave. Violet hit the cement with her elbow and curled up reflexively to protect her head from the stampede of legs and feet. Josh had stumbled over her and scrambling up, lifted her with him.

In the months of their new friendship, the world she had pulled around herself like a narrow corridor began to swell and pulse as they talked of civil rights, the war, military tycoonism, racism that had many faces. They saw and touched their common wounds.

Josh talked about his war. He who escaped the draft, his mother's endless work to help him through college, his father whose heart was crushed by the humiliation of worklessness. His father's death gave him life, the circumstance for exemption from the military, and the freedom to revolt, protest.

Violet talked about her war. The sheets of silence that covered history from the moment the gates slammed her parents into concentration camps in Arkansas. Her mother distant and forgetful. Her father demanding, critical. It didn't seem to matter what Violet achieved. They kept their silence like blades beneath their tongues.

Violet passed the old eucalyptus, branching high, its constant falling leaves and shedding bark making the air smell pungent. She noticed the green van, dismissed it in the glaring light of afternoon.

He crouched lower behind the wheel as she passed, seeing her closer, the dark sloping eyes, her olive skin browned by the sun, her delicate mouth and bones above her cheek. The beads of sweat popping around her brow.

They all had Vietnamese women.
None like mine.
She was bamboo thin,
her fingers clutching
the hem of her sleeve
like a child.
I felt red flame
licking the nape of my neck burning
deeper than napalm.
She was quiet,
her eyes, darker than night
helped me forget my My Lais.
Her beautiful body
curling around me,
flesh cocooned me against the
jungle where eyes were like rain.
Her arms like ivory bracelets
encircling my pain.
Flesh whole, sensual, shining
amidst the stench of rotting wounds
that fed the fat flies.
The insatiable flies of Vietnam.

Violet felt her anger draining with each step. The pounds shed, the tightening of her thighs, the new curves at her hips, and the thoughts of leaving home soon. Free as the wind in her face. Free from the jagged silences of her mother, the brooding disapproval of her father. Violet had informed them that she would be moving in with Josh. Perhaps they would live in Oregon where he was interviewing for a job at the University. She smiled, thinking of Josh's return, his sardonic grin when she told him of her parent's reaction. Josh who encouraged her to run, to strengthen herself. to speak her mind. to open her body, so long wrapped in years of suffocation. Her body that she had felt pitifully shapeless, small, powerless, burdened with blame and fault. If only he had not died. He was not due for another month. Her mother's face, pinched in pain as water and blood ran from her, rushed to the hospital. Her mother's body, wracked, gray, heaving and bellowing. The child tearing to exit too soon. She could still hear the screams from her mother's bones. The son, born dead. She remembered feeling alone. The weight of their grief, the sense of regret that she remained alive, on her small shoulders. All these years, the weight like boulders, the weight now shedding with each step.

The sun was a hot hand on her back as Violet ran through the threaded leaves, cracking beneath her steady feet.

He could feel the drugs wearing off. His skin twitching. He imagined the sores popping anew, the smell from jungle rot seeping from his pale flesh, tinted blue. He knew he would vomit.

> She never withheld her warm thighs,
> even when gorged with woman blood,
> hot blood
> sucking me deeper into her.
> All the blood that would fill
> a river.
> Those jungles, villages like
> a body split, slit, gouged.
> Blood on me.
> Swelling within her,
> my blade, gleaming in the moonlight
> exits flesh, flashes in her eyes.
> She licks the blood from the shaft.
> Deep, I thrust it past her teeth.
> She took it all
> her throat tightening on it
> blood bubbling from the edges
> of her lips.
> Her arms circling my hips,
> her hands moving in my groin
> with grenade.
> My blade cuts the arm away,
> splits her womb
> that spumes hot blood.

Violet noticed the day emptier, the sun hotter. No wind. She would reach her boulders today. Her mouth open slightly as she pushed her breath. The path became clearer, the trees very still. Like entering a strange new place. She remembered her corridor where she withdrew, compressed by whispers of guilt, mother's unhappiness, father's loneliness. Her narrow corridor, airless. Dark. Her flesh lined the walls. Josh's hands touching, warming her surfaces, expanding. His long runner's body entering her corners. Breathing. She discovers sensation. Muscles moving, sinews of desire. Nerve endings alive.

Violet stood before her parents and shouted. Her mother threatened to kill herself. Her father informed her she could never bring Josh into his house. It was bad enough to marry outside her race, but to live in sin with someone especially *that* color is endless disgrace. Violet's fury unleashed like exploding walls. She would leave this week. Run free of them. Lift it all from her like the wind picking up leaves and spinning them to the sky.

The son, blue and breathless, wrinkled like a raisin. Mother gave up back then, switched off her eyes. Her dull face all these years never saw her daughter's pain. Well, Violet didn't want to take it on anymore. Can't bring him back to life. Can't trade places, can't be what they want, no matter what she did. Had he lived, he'd be in college or a soldier drafted, maybe dead anyway in Southeast Asia.

Violet running faster. She'd live her own life. She could see the boulders now.

He, crouching behind the trees, watched her lengthening shadow climbing the boulder where she lay down, stretched her bare arms and legs glistening with sweat. Her body lifted by her panting breath.

He pulls her by both legs onto the ground. She is surprised. not knowing how she fell. He pulls her to him, hand over her mouth and drags her into the trees. Her legs are strong, digging into the soft earth, resisting, thrashing. He reveals the long knife unsheathed, whispers that he will cut her throat if she screams. Violet retreats into her corridor, breathing quietly through her nose. He leads her far from the path, under brush and thicket of trees. He commands her to kneel in the leaves. Violet, terror exploding, screams, her fists beating against his pressing body, suffocating, scarred, distorted flesh. He falls upon her like a rock. His fists beat her again, brutally again, until she is unconscious. He pulls her shorts off, and gently. Gently. Caressing, kisses her slightly open mouth, her neck, her still arms. Inserts his blade in her womb and makes her bleed.

After, he carefully dresses himself. With a wide arched swing of his sharp knife, he severs her arm above the elbow.

Wiping the blood from his blade, gently he wraps the arm in his flak jacket. Carries it like a child to his van and leaves.

The wind is still, the sun falling, casting long shadows from the boulders, the trees. In the thicket, the faint hum of flies gathering.

> Spirit of the bayonet.
> red/harch
> white/hup
> blue/eyes front
> Square your piece
> left/right
> kill 'em
> thrust/jab
> jab
> jab/kill 'em
> "hey mamasan
> joto mate ichiban"
> poontang one/two
> poontang three/four
> when we're done
> we'll kill some more.

Healthy Choices

Hold still

Keep quiet.

Get a degree
to learn how to talk
saying nothing.

Catch a good man
by being demure.
the one your mother chooses.

Let him climb you
whenever his urge,
amidst headaches
and menstrual aches
and screaming infants.
And when he bids
quick, turn over.

Hold still.

Make your tongue
a slab of cement
a white stone etched

with your name.
Kill your stories with knives
and knitting needles
and Clorox bleach.

Hide in your mysteriousness
by saying nothing.

Starch your thoughts
with ironed shirts.

Tie your anger
with a knot in
your throat
and when he comes
without concern,
swallow it.

Hold still.

Keep desire
hopeless as ice
and sleepless nights
and painful as a pinched eyelid.

Keep your fingers
from the razor,
keep your longing
to sever
his condescension
safely in your douchbag.

Turn the blade
against yourself.
Don't twitch
as your slashed wrists
stain your bathroom tiles.
Disinfect with Pine Sol.

Hold still.

Keep quiet.

Keep tight your lips,
keep dead your dreams,
keep cold your heart.

Keep quiet.

And he will shout
praises
to your
perfection.

The Lovers

The man came
in from the field.
He said nothing
to the woman
and began to eat
that which she prepared for him.
They moved,
carefully
inevitably
as the silent keeping
of time.

For them,
it moved nowhere
but to etch lines
on the woman's face,
the man's hands.
"The plums are small"
is all he said.
The woman,
facing the man,
speechless,
poured the steaming tea
slowly to half cup.
    (The steam,
    ghosting her vision,
    her desire
    her unspoken words:)

66

I will start with your
hands,
and slowly
with the sickle
slice the folds
of each finger
so blood will
form patterns
like the scales of fish.
Then I will hold the slivers
of flesh
and peel them slowly
as we do the skin of ripe
plums
until your eyes
widen with the pain
until the bone
appears like hope.
You will wince
as I approach
your face
with my razor sharp
fish knife
and carve your cheekbones
leaving only the flesh
around your eyebrows
shaped like wings.
And your eyes,
that are indifferent like the dead
will come alive
with horror/seeing me
for the first time.

Listen, listen
I will whisper
to the rhythm of your blood

rippling like the river
that feeds your plums.

The man gazes up
at her,
    (she is straddling him
    with the blade between her teeth
    a love never seen before
    in his smile)
he does not smile.
    (and he will say:)

        I hear the singing of plums
        drinking the earth,
        sucking the sun.
        You have kept your breasts
        hidden from me
        in darkness.
        I could only feel
        the ripe smooth bursting
        as I entered
        the root place
        between your thighs.
        Silence has been my defense
        of your woman masterhood.

        The trees are my friends.
        What they ask of me,
        I can give.
        What I plant
        I get back.
        What I nourish
        I eat.
        Entering the house
        with you in your silent

making
your suffocating
servitude,
I will pull with my strong neck
the plow blade,
you, like the shaft of wheat
slipping to the threshing
floor
scattered there like seed.
I will run the blade
first up the sides
of your thighs
until your blood
has grained the wood.

The woman, wordless,
pours his tea
silently.

The man,
eyes indifferent like the dead
says,
"The plums are small
this year."

Fats

I should've gotten mad.

I must be getting old.

Children
waste like cornflakes
in a milkless tenderloin room,
carried off by
rats
that are everywhere,
getting fat.

Fats got himself stuck
in the plumbing.
Died. Decaying.
Water running through
his corpse.

Pregnant women drink,
children wet their cornflakes.

I get sick.

I must be getting old.

70

WHAT MATTERS

What Matters

The things that matter
you ask, where is love?
The poem
soft as linen
dried by the sun?
words of comfort
like puffed pillows
yellow flowers
with velvet petals?
Where is serenity,
cherry blossoms arranged,
the quaint ceremony of tea?
Images metaphysically deep
spoken in Japanese,
preferably seventeen syllables
of
persimmons or new
plums or snow covered bridges
or red flow of leaves?
What matters
the trickling clarity of
water
each day, not fearing thirst.
                I love you
when persimmons sweat
shining in a sand gray bowl,
                Mama
hiding pennies
under floor boards

with flour, saltine crackers,
balls of used aluminum foil,
string, coupons and water jars
secreted for that day.
That day
when all would be taken
and packing
must be quick again.
      I love you
when snow covers the bridge
curved over ice white water
          Grandfather
killing my cat
who ripped open his hens,
sucking their eggs.
His eyes, half closed
behind steel rims,
cigarette holder
clenched in his teeth,
as he fondled the rock.
Before I could cry
or plead,
my cat, writhing
with skull crushed.
He captured a rabbit,
gave it to me
and warned
we would eat in winter
as soon as I began to love her.

      I love you
when plums burst like new moons,
crescents on their black boughs
         my husband
whose dark hands
embrace the wilted shoulders
of the wretched,
winos with wracked eyes,
and welfare mothers cleaning cockroaches

from the lips of their children.
His words
like spoons, nourishing.
          I love you
when leaves flow in crimson,
orange, yellow, sepia waves
          my daughter
who weeps for each dead
seal, murdered tiger,
cat's corpse, endangered species
of condor and chinese panda,
crusading against gamesmen
and trophy hunters.
          What matters,
Breath
for the shipwrecked, drowning.
          What matters
amidst the dread of nuclear winter,
Chernobyl's catastrophe, Three Mile Island,
Nevada's test veterans, terrorism,
the massacred in Port Elizabeth, the
wounded of Central America, genocide of drugs,
AIDS, toxic waste, Atlanta's missing
and mutilated, hunger, mistaken identities,
murder in the streets.
          A love poem?

          Clear water passing   (5)
          our mouths unafraid to breathe,   (7)
          and to speak freely.   (5)

Graciella

Graciella's arms,
big like hammocks
swaying mounds of work,
her eyes like moons
moving the waves
of soil   breaking
bursting green leaves
iceberg lettuce.

>   and he watched
>   from the shade of his elm,
>   pleased.

From her body
glistened
wires of water across
her face,
her big arms
cradled the work,
her hands like a weaver,
threading the dirt
to a rich, dark rug
until the sun fell
behind the elm.

>   best damned worker
>   I ever had,
>   good as a dozen wetbacks
>   even with the kid
>   strapped
>   to her back he said, pleased.

From her body
she pushed a child
head swollen
veins rippling
from his hairless skull
>   no work, no pay
>   she doesn't miss a day
>   they push 'em out like rabbits
>   he said, pleased.

Into her body
she sucked the sun,
the soil, into her fingers
her pores,
into her nostrils,
her throat
the white chemical dust
sprayed from the cropduster
into her blood
that ran through her child
who died writhing like a hooked worm.

She did not work
that day.
>   Displeased,
>   he docked her pay.

>   He did not offer
>   her child's grave
>   to be planted in the shade
>   of his elm.

Assaults and Invasions

Linette was beaten daily.
He said she wasn't any good, dumb and weak even for a woman.

Every time I'd see her, face swollen like a bruised soft peach, lip hanging big and purple over her chin, her eyes bled hunger and helplessness. When he would start in on her, she could only defend with fingernails and sweat and a tongue fat with broken veins and angry words. She is a hundred and five pounds powerless to his two hundred pound body, and she opens her legs like murdered wheat. She moved out several times, this time reporting him to the police, begged the courts to restrain him. He found her, and when she wouldn't whimper or cry or open her thighs this time, he with his razor began to slice small slivers of flesh from her breasts, her crotch, her belly, like scaling a fish, until her body bubbled like a red carp. Her mouth so thick with pain, she could hardly scream stop it. stop it. stop it.

Today, United States Marines invade Grenada. Why do I think of this woman's life? Like sirens that hurt the ears of dogs, like insidious water dripping through rusty drains, like the pain of flesh slowly slivered and peeled, we want to scream, stop it.

Yesterday, Benigno Aquino, bringing hope home like a day full of poppies, died. Undisguised murder in the open air, his blood darkening into tunnels of the earth. Marcos' assassins pick their teeth, and the day spills the stench of rotten fish. We beat our fists against the windows, weeping in the passageways...stop it.

Linette barely lived. The police did nothing. The courts shrugged their shoulders and yawned. When she went home from the hospital, he was waiting, enraged by her acts of defiance. He took his razor and burning cigarette and made her hurt, made her bleed. She knew this time he would show he could control her death. She wanted to survive. The bullet went through his heart, and she thought she saw for the first time in his eyes, surprise that she had made him stop it.

So why do I think of this woman on the day of the invasion in Grenada?

We cannot catch our breath, our tongues too thick with rage, beating our fists against windows. Each day people disappear in Chile, Paraguay, Honduras, Uruguay, Bolivia, Guatemala. Assaults against the sovereignty of Nicaragua. Blockades against Cuba, genocide in El Salvador. Murders in Manila. Apartheid in South Africa.

Each day the ism's like a boot attempt to crush us: racism, capitalism, imperialism, materialism, sexism, colonialism, ageism, classism, militarism.

> We must breathe deeply.
> Escape through the windows.
> We must gather, find each other.
> Hear the heartbeats, the power in our veins.
> We must clear our voices,
> take action to make ourselves known.
> We must stop it
> stop it
> stop it.

Red

For rent.

I watched
the chickens circle,

scratching
out their code.

One of the rules
of the yard
was to keep
the red birds
away from the white flock.

She,
combed neat,
peeked
from shaded windows.

The Red
had flown from her coop
where she was kept
apart,   now
surrounded by
the flock.

She,
sharp eyed
and lidless,
cooed
from the crack
of her door,

There aren't any of you
in this neighborhood.

        The flock rushes
        and Red
        is buried beneath
        white feathers flying.
        Red's
        head bleeding.
        Beaks plucking, pecking
        crazed by blood.

        Old Red. Dead.

        Didn't know her place.

"...If You Don't
Want to Believe It..."

Coffee steaming,
my daughter asleep
safely in the morning.
There are trees outside
that bloom here.
Wind brushes the begonias
dusting mist from
their eyes.
The sun slides
through my blinds
like razors.

Dateline, Johannesburg.
Soldier shoots a nine year old
black child in Soweto.
He thought he was shooting a dog.

A state of emergency.
Toaster burns out,
refrigerator broken,
these gadgets tied to my hands
not to comprehend
wholesale detention, slaughter.
The easy distraction of the blender,
tending of gardens.

A black child
dead.

Newsprint flickers
over the sea, the mountains,
the plains of drying bones,
blood flecked corrugated
iron fences.

A black child is dead.
He thought it was a dog.

Dead black child.
Lucifer's smile,
like dead light
with all the care of diamonds
wrapped to our fingers.

Dead black child
mistaken for a dog.
The official response:
"...if you don't want to believe it,
you don't have to."

His smile glinting like
the cold white stones in his mines.

(Quote from South African Government spokesman,
San Francisco Chronicle, June 21, 1986.)

Where Is Beauty, Imelda?

Imelda Marcos says: "Power and strength is man. Beauty, inspiration, love is woman. Women have their place in the home, in the bedroom..."

Where is beauty, Imelda?

Your heart is dead winter
your words like mouldy cake
undernourishing us.

You, a rancid rose,
withered petals between your thighs.

Where is inspiration?

Your rivers have dried.
The horses are thirsty.

The man you prop on a throne is straw,
swollen from cirrhosis.

He does not remember
his own lies.

Your legs close tightly
clutching the refuse
of your country.

Children steal rotting fruit, paper, plastic.
They hunger
like the weather, a beggar that rips
the skin off mangos and defiles
them in the sun.

Your hills are naked, taut
like the people, seedless.

Where is love?

Decadence in the palace.
You dare not open your thighs.
The smell will kill the gardenias
floating in your opulent gardens.

The business of the bedroom, Imelda,
with assassins and aging generals
whose cheeks bloat with fear,
whose fingers shake
and drying flesh chatters
in the wind growing
over darkening mountains.

How will you lock
your bedroom?

How will you conceal

bones of the murdered
sprouting like trees?

How will you stop

the strength of thunder
gathering in villages?

How will you explain

the power
of rain
that washes your refuse
from the shouting streets?

Serafin

You would be proud.

Once you said
yellow was your favorite color
    (next to brown).

We remember your poems
to farmworkers
and manongs
to the murdered and the hungry
of your homeland.

You sang
even with your pain
    (the pain that took you from us)
plucking at you
between your eyes.

Serafin,
the yellow is vast
surging like fields of
buttercups and jonquils
shouting Cory. Cory. Cory.

The Marcos' are gone.
Ferdinand is stuttering

in an empty room.
Imelda speaks and we are
astounded. Amused. She insists all those
shoes belong to the maid.
She sings
to an empty room.

You would be proud.
A woman leads your people.
Cory is strong.
She reminds us of our mothers
who want to fill our stomachs.
She speaks wisely to our enemies.
Her smile is kind.

Look Serafin...
All the yellow
clad brown people,
brilliant as the day,
as the hope
that shines from
your poems
about the revolution
that has come.

Love Canal

And you will forget
even this

        the earth
        gray, its sickness
        bubbling
        through the cracked lips
        of packed dirt.
        Maria
        lays in her bed
        lined with mourners,
        suitors, priests, sons.
        In love,
        her eyes dropping
        sorrow,
        her pale gray hands
        thinned to the bone
        fingering the beads,
        hope emaciated like starved
        women.
        Maria,
        mother, lover.
        opening for them
        like a moist cave
        promising tomorrow,
        forever.

And you will forget
even this.

They wound
the heart,
burn, pierce,
bludgeon the breast
of Love Canal.
Her lips, lungs swell,
heave, spit
Maria dreams
between her pain,
her skin burning,
cells screaming
armpits glowing
with bright embers
of radiation treatments.
He brought sunshine
like marigolds
into her lap
made her heart pump full
with rhythms of a young colt.
And in the streams
surrounding Love Canal,
they would dip, sip,
deep into each other's skin.
Her body
a canal for love
glistens with pain
sores like water
running to the edges of
her flesh.

And you will forget
even this

Hooker Chemical Company
pours the poison
dumps its waste

into vessels of earth
at Love Canal.
Mothers sip
from its wells,
children sleep
in the fragrant air
of buried waste,
fathers infertile
hum lullabys to unborn.
Maria awakens
from her toxic pillow
wet from the canal
of her polluted body,
flesh aflame,
bubbling pain,
like the angry earth
spewing sickness.

The priests and suitors
pray   fear no evil
                fear no evil
                fear evil
                evil...
over her body
once Love's Canal.

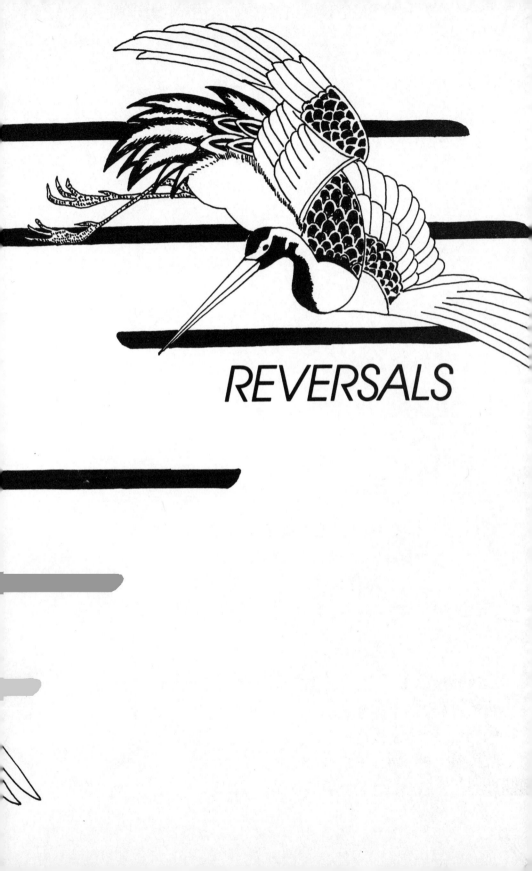

REVERSALS

Reversals

For Layne

I find myself
now, sending
you words on yellow paper
to share my void,
the fears, the small complaints
that make hairline
wrinkles around my mouth.
I remember
when we searched
as children
in the fields,
in the abandoned
fallen chick houses,
I for insects
to pin to my collection,
my insects, neatly pinned
guarded against you,
in the convent of my room.
Your search
for the streak of gold
in rocks,
black little stones,
joyful, envied by me.
You seemed so fearless
of loss or failure.

A stone cast aside,
worthless, quickly forgotten,
while I,
as if to gather small, irreplaceable
bits of myself,
would stockpile
broken wings,
dismembered limbs
and carefully add
to my collection.
My brother,
I did not know
your manhood would not consume
my barren room,
impaled with dead butterflies.
Nor that your capacity
for joy, your ease
with life
could streak gold
on this small stone,
my heart.

Zipper

Stolen breath,
groping in corners,
closets,
barn,
darkened bedrooms while all
is hushed
by sleep
or distance,
his fingers search
the length of her body,
muffled in disgust, fear.
Puberty swelling
in small breasts, squeezed
like spring pears.
Don't.

as the zipper presses
along white mound of bone,
soft flesh.
His tongue flicks to wet
dry lips.
His fingers work the shiny zipper.
No silent prayer,
no whisper of disgrace,
no speechless pain
would keep the teeth
clenched. Zipper
undone.
A jagged sneer across her flesh.

Jade

The woman insisted
my name must be Jade.
Your name's not Jade?
Well, it should be.
It suits you, jewel of the orient.

I knew a young hooker
called Jade.
She had red dyed hair
and yellow teeth
bucked around a perpetual candy bar.
They called her Jade
because she was Clyde's
jewel of the orient.
Her real name was Sumiko...
Hardy or Johnson or Smith.
She was from Concord.
Boring, she said,
and kept running away
from home. Her father
would come looking for her,
beat her again,
drag her home
while her mother
babbled and bawled in Japanese.
Concord was boring.
Jade kept running away,

Clyde's jewel of the orient.
He took care of her well,
and she couldn't wait
to see him, her hunger
like locusts in drought,
to put the cold needle to her vein,
blood blossoming in the
dropper like bougainvillea
pushing the heroin through,
her eyes exploding with green lights,
the cold encasing
each corpuscle,
rushing through
heart to the spine,
a freeze settling in each
vertebrae until
she's as cold as stone,
metabolism at zero degrees,
speech center numbed
and life as still as icicles.
Pain, boredom, loneliness
like a frosty pillow
where she lays her nodding
head.

          I wanted to tell
          the woman who kept
          insisting my name was Jade
about Jade.
who od'd. Her jaundiced body
found on her cold floor
mattress,
roaches crawling in her ears,
her dead eyes, glassy
as jewels.

Who Is Singing
This Song?

<blockquote>
I am
</blockquote>

The Oi River
winding around fields
full with rice waving
bursting with women planting.
I leave with spurts of wind
spilling to the Pacific
great passageway for small boats.

Who is singing this song?

<blockquote>
I am
</blockquote>

The water and air
that dances
on your fingertips,
the water swirling in precise pools
that slake your thirst,
water with tempo, measure,
murmur, licking at your ear.

Who is singing this song?

<blockquote>
I am
</blockquote>

A street veering, connecting
colliding with corners
rolling up/down hills.

Smell me.
rice/adobo
sashimi
imo/juk/gai lon
kimchee.

Hear me.

We survive by hearing.

Who is singing this song?

                    I am

We discover each other
our small silences peel open
like roses
We explore the layers of our fears.
                will he   will I   will they   will I not?

We have so long undressed without light
ashamed of our size
the shape of our thighs
the sweep of our eyes.

We survive by hearing

We ignite ourselves from inside

The light surrounds us and we
are surprised.

I seek where and how to touch.

Who is singing this song?

I am

The hands of grandmother, mother
sinewed from work,
blue veined like magnolias
soft as cloth, wiping away
the sweat from men's shoulders
massaging the balms, the lotions
deep into their backs.

I look through family albums
the women's hands clasped like small bouquets,
Umeko, plum blossom child.
Shigemi, luxurious growth of beauty.
Haruko, beautiful spring.
Minoru, treasured son, bearer of fruit.

These hands have yielded me,
palms open, allowing birth,
tying cord, pulling knot
through immigration,
segregation, tribulation,
relocation.

Who is singing this song?

I am

a floating note on a koto
a thunderstorm steady like taiko
I can be heard humming the blues
in rice paddies
and desert camps, unraveling barbed wire
like silkworm thread.

A woman
dancing in the ocean's swell
searching for pearls in the pacific
I string them across my eyes,
my skin the color of moonlight.

I am your own, a child in dark streets,
woman seeking safety in a world of shadows,
I am the present, struggling to be free
a crusader in these spiritless prisons,
pinnacles to greed and sterility.

Who is singing this song?

I am

a survivor
a saboteur of stereotypes
image maker, an endless string of speech.

We survive by hearing.

We discover each other
each of us yielded by hands
of the transplanted,
the escapees, the adventurers
pregnant with dreams.

We explore our similar histories.

We ignite ourselves from inside.

Our hands are warmed, alive.

Who is singing this song?

                    I am

pulled by hands of history
to not sit in our times,
complacently, walkmans plugged to our ears,
computer printouts, soap operas lulling us to sleep.

We are required by these hands of history
to be a storm of hands
that wave in protest
against apartheid, assaults,
invasions, indifference to the poor.

a storm of hands that
dismantle the MX's and the
Tridents and the Pershings and the Cruise missiles.

Who is singing this song?

                    I am

a river of hands that reach
to the suffering, the suppressed in
South Africa,
the paralyzed in El Salvador,
the starving of Ethiopia, the dying Hibakusha.

a wreath of hands
woven from blossoms shaped from
whispers for justice
over the grave of Vincent Chin.

a sea of beating hands
that persuade patriarchies that
strength is not force
and real power is not oppressing
nor patronizing,
but shared power
among people free, working,
creating, passionate.

Who is singing this song?

                    I am

We survive by hearing.
We speak to each other.

offering choices

to live, to dream
to extend our hands, to dance
to cringe, to quiver
to kiss, to not kiss.

I dare you
dare you

to love, to dream
to kiss.

We survive by hearing

Who is singing this song?

               I am.

Mama went to Hawaii
for her vacation.
Visited Pearl Harbor.
Brought back bad memories she says,
being Japanese.
Internment camps.

> Diamond Head.
> Polynesian Fantasy.
> Hibiscus Buffet.
> Fire dances.
> Aloha Festival.
> Having a great time.

Pearl Harbor.
Tired me out.

"When There Is Talk of War," a fictional prose piece, was inspired by the true story of a Japanese American "Hibakusha"—an atomic bomb survivor who, it is said, went for 30 years without feeling human touch. Because of the unknown nature of radiation sickness then, she feared contaminating her family and friends.

Unlike the survivors of Japan, Japanese American survivors who were trapped in Japan during World War II when the bombs were dropped and who subsequently returned to their homes in the United States, have often been isolated, victimized by the callous neglect of an American government that spent millions on research and construction of nuclear weapons, but nothing on its consequences—including medical research, medical compensation and other support systems.

When There Is
Talk of War

I know I am dying soon. In and out I float like a boat lifted on the shoulders of the sea, pain cresting high like white-capped waves. How many nights I want to let my body slide over the edge into dark, undulating arms, promising nothing.

Teru enters my room with a tray of steaming soup. How strange his smooth-fingered touch. My son, are you not tired of nursing this old woman? Are you not angry with the smell of death, Teru, clinging onto your youthful fingers, permeating this house full with your children?

Remember me once robust and full chested with the juices of health? The day you were born, your father hung blue paper fish, rejoicing that you were a boy. How proud I was I had made him so happy. Your father. Ah, how he would look at me, back then, with love. And the days rippled with joy, like the waves of the fields, as we worked side by side. Sometimes, desire would rise in me so strongly, I would grasp his dirt brown hands and pull him to the watershed where he would hold me. His kisses would linger like cool breezes until the work was done.

Ah, Teru, I remember him too well, and my bed is cold and painful and empty. The tongue of death has licked this wasted body, gutted by memories of dead fish, falling flesh, hair floating in flame, ashes of Hiroshima.

This cruel death wraps me in rasping breath, negating all else...nothing else matters...only the reality of this pain. Those things which you feel so strongly about, my son, with the idealism of your youth, like peace and justice...are nothing.

Where was justice that day when my visit to Hiroshima marked the beginning of my suffering, this solitary journey to my grave? Where was justice that day so long ago when innocent ones vaporized, burned, scattered in an instant blaze? Where was justice that hot day in August when death dropped like giant broken wings, sweeping all within its broken flight? A thousand suns soaked into our palms. Memory followed as endless rivers, black with bodies, soaked with weeping. Water turned to vinegar, disbelief, mercilessness.

But I am too tired for bitterness and regret...I have only this desire for it to be ended now. I must put those years of hospitals and grim faced medical men behind me, those answerless years of wait and worry.

I want to give you something before I die, my son, that is whole and fresh like the trees outside my window—not this waste of body, this moan I can't suppress, this smell of slow decay. I want to leave you with the memory of me lifting your childbody, carrying you joyfully like a basket of plump radiant peaches from our orchard, blossoms swirling like songs, trees swaying like women in love.

I am wrong, Teru, I have one regret. This throat of death sucking without comfort...for thirty years I would not touch you nor your father for fear you would catch this then unknown disease, and I would weep those endless nights with loneliness and fury because I could not cradle my grandchildren, nor laugh with them on my lap, nor kiss their plump faces. Yes, I regret those years empty with not touching, not knowing. Those endless tests. Those endless costs...my body ravaged slowly by the cancer of that bombing, they say so now. All those years I could have been comforted by holding your face in my hands, my son. When your father died, I blamed myself. I am so tired, Teru, I wish I could smell the trees outside, or sleep without this pain.

Yes, I am wrong again, my son. Forgive me, but pain makes me so selfish. Peace and justice do matter. If my wasted body speaks nothing else, my son, *remember it when there is talk again of war. Add your single voice to remind them of my grandchildren who have lived with the smell of death. When there is talk again of war, remind them of the blackened mouths of sad dead women; remind them of the hands in flames reaching to a mute heaven; remind them of the cemeteries, the headstones of all our friends; the water filled with dead fish, the poisoned rains. When there is talk again of war, remind them of the absent ones, remind them of our wasted flesh.* Not out of bitterness, my son, but out of compassion. Not for me, my son, but for my grandchildren.

The sleep comes now, like no other. Your father is on this ship that rides my waves. The distance between us lessens. He has waited as he did in the furrows of our fields, thirsting for my lips and the cool drink I have made for him. I cannot mend my past and my present, now as thin as a wing's membrane. Perhaps you can, my son. I will touch the smile that hides in the corners of your mouth this last time. I will not cry for those years we spent at distance. I will only hear the peach trees swaying like women in love. My body is billowing on the great shoulder of this sea, and I join your father, brilliant as a thousand suns that burn into this, my darkness.

For Jeannine

Autumn comes
like a buyer of cloth,
her long fingers
touching,
turning orange,
yellow, brown.

taking what she wants,
stretching
the bone taut air.

Her skin crackles beneath
our feet.

          I didn't think anyone wanted me,

bruises pulled
like a sweater around
my neck.

We talk
in the pore tightening air,
branches bare,
about the girl buried in the chill
of prewinter.

We show each other
our mutilated children
in the guise of women
as autumn plucks
at our lips.

Each color,
blue, black, ochre
popping like kisses
on the rib lined flesh,
the puberty soft thighs.

And we muse
how women
keep bruises
hidden
beneath dead
leaves.

Jealousy

is a man's prerogative,
a measure of his manhood,
proof of his love for the woman.

jealousy

is forbidden for a woman,
an ungracious emotion
punishable with shame, guilt,
a measure of her insecurity.

When a man is jealous
it is the woman's fault.
She is bitch for causing him self-
doubt or pain, for daring to challenge
his dominion.

When a woman is jealous
it is the woman's fault
for not being attractive/intelligent/charming/
thin enough. Worse, she is manipulative,
controlling, possessive, castrating,
destructive.

Jealous women have been called evil.

Who told us?

      our fathers? the psychiatrist?
      a lecherous uncle? Mother?

Do they lie?

Do they lie.

Tearing Threads

Slowly,

light enters
like gauze spilling
on her shoulders.

She sees for the first time
the aging pools beneath his eyes,
the crippled words
from his thinning lips.

It was not she who
caused him to leave.
She who thought herself unlovable,
unworthy.

She remembered
in her bones,
in the fibres of her skin
how she waited
by the telephone
for years, waiting
until she fell asleep
with cords and threads
and distances wrapped
around her throat.

The agony
was the silence,
cruel silence
of unringing telephones,
unanswered mail.

She began to put on layers
of cloth
to keep herself warm.

She read poems about dead fathers
by Sylvia Plath,
stayed close to the oven.

Each year,
another fabric layered
over another
just as her mother
whose lips
were covered by scarves.

She believed
this penance
required of unlovable women.

Today,

sight restored,
she removes her coat.

He is not giant,

hero, king of life
who she created
who could bestow
the gift of happiness,
acceptance.

Simply an aged man
who ran
to the good times,

forgetting the pain
of old cages made from barbed wire
and dust and potato skins
and arranged marriages,

escaping to
the laughter
of good times,

a well-told joke
discreetly whispered,
withheld from the ears
of children.

She unknots her scarves,
the shawls,
the quilted squares
tied together over her arms.

This loosening of garments,
tearing of thread,
uncovering each layer,

revealing her bare skin,
her lips

shedding
shedding

the silence.

Why Is Preparing Fish
A Political Act?

Preparing fish
each Oshogatsu
I buy a gleaming rock cod,
pink, immaculately gutted.
Each year, a respectable fish
that does not satisfy
(hard as I try)
to capture flavors
once tasted.

Grandmother's hands
washing, scaling, cleaning
her fish,
saved each part,
guts, eggs, head.
Her knife, rusted
at the handle screws
ancient as her curled fingers.
Her pot, dented,
darkened, mottled with age
boiled her brew
of shoyu
sweetened with ginger and
herbs she grew
steamed with blood, water.
Nothing wasted.

Someone once tried to sell her
a set of aluminum
pots, smiling too much, called her
mamasan.
Her silence thicker than
steaming shoyu,
whiter than sliced bamboo root
boiled with fish heads.

Preparing fish
is a political act.

Shedding Silence

Grandfather: Tsuki ga, deta deta...
                *(Grandfather dances on
                stage, singing traditional
                folk song.)*
                Bon.
                Festival of the Dead.
                Fires light the heat of August.
                Lanterns guide us home.
                Dancers in flowered kimonos
                circle, with drum, flute.
                Smells of barbeque teriyaki,
                sake spilling from barrels.
                All the spirits stop
                to watch
                young girls with brown skin
                bare in summer dresses.
                Old men stretch their necks
                to sing the high notes...
                        Tsuki ga, deta deta
                        Tsuki ga, deta yoi yoi.
                Taiko
                steady as heartbeats
                powerful as thunder.

Chieko: Shina no yoru...
                *(Chieko enters. She is singing
                "China Nights". She is dressed
                in white kimono with sea-
                green undergarment. Trailing
                from her hands is a bright*

crimson obi with gold and silver chrysanthemums woven in the silk. She is beautiful, pale, hair neatly combed into traditional Japanese style, held with lacquer combs and wisteria flowers. Grandfather catches the end of the obi, holds it taut as Chieko wraps it around herself.)

Chieko:

Bon Odori
Dance for the Dead.
      Shina no yoru, yo...
Obi will tie
around my breasts
wrap tightly my joy,
my sorrow.
Obi will still my fury.
Knot at my heart.
Threads woven
into fine cloth
slashes across my waist,
layer over layer
pulled tight,
tighter,
to conceal my body
thin as a reed,
hollowed, scraped, whittled.
Inside, fermenting flesh,
spoiled fruit the color
of a scraped womb.
Inside, milk souring,
standing water.
I am the song
of the obi,
contained, confined.
Under the binding of silk
are suffocated
wild horses, yellow volcanos,

riverbanks thick with red flowers,
the wind, sleeping in caves.
   Shina no yoru...
   I will pour tea,
display my skills
at various ceremony.
My voice and art of dance
will turn the heads
of all men.
One brave warrior
will pause,
sleep in the wide waves
of my kimono sleeves,
and I will comfort him
with my sacrifice...
   (She laughs, her voice too
   shrill)
See, Sansei.
It isn't easy.
   (Chieko floats off stage,
   humming "China Nights".
   Her obi is tightly in place,
   tied with a wide bow at her
   waist. Grandfather sits on
   a short stool, in almost a
   squatting position. The spot
   is on his face, made up
   white, an almost mask like
   quality.)

Grandfather: Bon.
Festival of the Dead.
Everyone comes home
gathered for a feast.
The women prepare
norimaki. Teriyaki chicken.
Potato salad.
Corn on the cob.
Sashimi gleaming moist and fresh
in boats of lotus leaves.

Everyone is home
travelling long distances.
Russell, grandson,
Jadine, granddaughter.
Tosh, my drunken son.
Haru, father of my grandchildren.
Michi, my daughter, wife of Haru.
My old wife, lighting incense at the altar,
whispers prayers for me and my poor
daughter, Chieko.
Hiro, grandson, listens to spiders.

> *(Spot comes up on the shape*
> *of Hiro, sitting crosslegged*
> *near his grandfather, in*
> *front of a window. We*
> *cannot see his face or size.)*

Hiro: Spiders more fun than anything.
Stretching white threads
across my window.
Waits for flies and moths.
Mommy knits, waiting always
for daddy, who works into the night.
Soon a moth
with red eyes, flies to the window.
Spider quick, bites moth.
Wraps it up for dinner.
Grandmother say never kill spider.
Might kill Grandfather's soul
or Auntie Chieko's.
Spider is ghost of ancestors, spinning
stories in their webs.

> *(Chieko floats back on stage)*

Chieko: Thread
spinning, spinning
into obi,
wrapped tightly,
a reminder to mince steps/words.
Take shallow, quick breaths,

release your sorrow
discreetly, drop by small drop.
>
> *(She pulls out a fan and
> begins her dance, position-
> ing the fan coyly in front of
> her face, flutters it across
> her body)*

He said my beauty was delicate
like ginkgo leaves, small fans
in the wind.
Grace. That's what it's all about.
Grace in failure, in times of need.
Fall gracefully.
Die graciously, quickly
in a cold, white moment.
Because without love,
we are nothing.
Without love
we wither into clumsy uprooted stumps,
cluttering and offensive
to those who need to
get somewhere in a hurry.
>
> *(She laughs again, too shrill)*

I tell you, Sansei.
It isn't easy.
>
> *(Chieko dances to opposite
> side of stage from grand-
> father. She sits on a stool,
> gracefully, posed. Her face
> like a mask, spotted. Lights
> focus on a family dining
> room table, where Jadine
> and Russell are alone
> together.)*

Jadine:	So, how's your life, Russ?
Russell:	I'm in love.
Jadine:	Again?
Russell:	She's a dream.
Jadine:	What color?
Russell:	What difference does it make?

Jadine:	Oh. I see.
Russell:	We don't see each other for a year. Still into being *political?*
Jadine:	Does she tell you how much she loves our flower arranging? And those clever little radios we make so well?
Russell:	Not funny, Jay.
Jadine:	Remember the last one you were in love with who expected me to wash her dishes and let Ma wait on her like we were her maids?
Russell:	What the hell's wrong with you?
Jadine:	I ain't white. Don't you know, baby, I got an inferiority complex.
Russell:	Goddam right.
Jadine:	What does she tell you to do, prune her bush, *gardener?*
Russell:	She happens to think I'm a pretty good surgeon. Hey. Sound bitter, sis. Gonna shrivel you up. Unbecoming.
Jadine:	I've never been "becoming" to you, bro.
Russell:	Yeah. I know you. You possessed. A demon of self-hate. You think your looks don't get you over so you gotta compete with me. Kill me, overachiever. Your competence suffocates me. You make me feel...small. Who wants that?
Jadine:	You feel equal to a white woman, boy? She got her satin slipper on your neck.
Russell:	If I'm gonna get castrated, better a white woman. They're *supposed* to control us.

(Russell walks out. Angry. Pushes over a chair. In the backdrop, slides are projected as if on a t.v. screen. Vogue *covergirl. Voluptuous* Cosmopolitan *model. Calvin Klein jean ad. Lights dim, single spot on Jadine. She speaks in flashback, out to the audience.)*

Jadine:	I had a crush on this white guy, see? He was a track star. Drove a blue convertible and had gray eyes. He dated my roommate in college. Becky Blomquist. God I envied her. One day the track star calls up, I answer, tell him Becky's not home. And he says he's calling me. Well, I'm shocked. But I told him I'd meet him in the back of the library. Wanted all my buddhahead friends to see me walking off with him. When he picks me up, the buddhaheads are snickering. I think, yellow with envy. Me and gray eyes in his blue convertible. He parks near the tennis courts, deserted and dark. Starts kissing me. The night sounds stopped. The air started smelling of jasmine and silver stars. It was really something. His hands start up my sweater and he kisses my breasts. My sweater comes up over my head. Suddenly all the white lights go on. It was crazy, like a bomb had dropped and I just didn't hear it. I look at him and he's smiling like nothing's happening. I grab for my sweater and bra and I hear the laughter now like red rain. Three of his friends from the track team turned on all the big tennis court lights and he is laughing too. Said they never made it before with a yellow chick and couldn't I take a joke?

(Spot on Chieko)

Chieko:	Bind, knot each thread.

Each stitch in our soul, a scar.
Gook
slopehead
jap
chink
tight eyes
dragon lady
geisha girl.

Don't speak of it.
Pull, wind,
wrap, tie the terror in your throat.
Choke without sound.
Secretly with fingers of genmai,
bonsai breeder,
cherry blossom breath.
Our arms will spin
these silent strings.

(Michi enters dining table set)

Michi: What's between you and your brother.
Fighting again?

Jadine: No. It's a joke.

Michi: Why are you so difficult?

Jadine: You mean why do I say what I think?

Michi: There are things best not said at all.

Jadine: You are so protective of your
precious son.
I will not act as you wish me to.

Michi: You could be attractive.

Jadine: Not on your terms.

Michi: You must learn, women are vulnerable.

Jadine: You are my beautiful mother.
Gracious under insult.
Firmly rooted in marriage and family.

Michi: Don't be sarcastic.
Beauty leaves with the years.
Mouths are everywhere, sucking at you.
Like the lips of air, drying you up.

Jadine: Beauty and youth should not be
everything for a woman.

Michi: You are not getting younger. We are
nothing without a man.

Jadine: What if I never find a man?

Michi: Then you are nothing.

Jadine: Fear sucks at you.

Michi: Woman is the farm. She lays as a field
and all things enter. The rain,
the frost, the sun.

	And we bear.
	All the slopes and valleys of us
	are tilled.
	Peeled open. Excavated. **Penetrated.**
	And we reproduce.
	This is what we do.
Jadine:	But I am a river.
	Frozen on its surface.
Michi:	The river still flows beneath.
Jadine:	We are afraid for anyone to come
	too close to us,
	afraid they will crack us open
	and we will drown them.
Michi:	You do not resemble me at all.
Jadine:	I am not your monument, your legacy.
	Do you not long for someting that
	is your own?
	That has been made by your hands,
	the light from your passion,
	the fire from your imagination?
	Something of you?
Michi:	No, you are not my monument.
	My son is.

(Dark)
(Spot on Grandfather,
Chieko)

Grandfather:	Man and woman
	like rock and water.
	Water must flow around rock.
	Eventually, wears it to sand.
Chieko:	Women, dangled
	from thread,
	rope.
	Wrapped in smothering cloth
	to hide our openings,
	our shoreless heart.
	We are locks without keys,
	a convent wall,
	a saltless sea.

(Dark)
(Lights up on Russell and Tosh)

Russell:	That stuff will kill you.
Tosh:	*(Waving his bottle)* Smart boy. Teach you that in medical school?
Russell:	Well, it's *your* liver.
Tosh:	My liver loves it. My ahtama *(pointing to his head)* loves it. And it loves me. Better than a woman.
Russell:	Your batteries dead, unc?
Tosh:	Hey. It's festival time, boy. She gives me a good time *(waves bottle)* She lets me sleep. Lets me say what I want to say. Doesn't ask for more than I'm willing to give. Doesn't nag me with guilt or weakness. She don't terrify me with purity, or threaten to withhold her body. She don't require performance or perfection. She lets me sleep.
Russell:	We climb out of their bellies worn, little old men. Even when we beat them, they try to make us feel strong. Coax us up again. Try to make us feel safe so we'll climb back in.
Tosh:	Life's dangerous, boy. Women can mix you up. They scream about wanting indepedence, but complain when you leave them alone. They say they want respect, but get mad when you don't come on strong. They call us self-centered when we tell them what to do but despise us for being weak when we ask them what they want.
Russell:	Pass the bottle, unc.

(Dark on Russell and Tosh. Lights up on women who are preparing sushi. Michi ladles steaming rice into a large bowl, pours sweet vinegar, stirring it into the rice. Jadine is cooling the

*vinegared rice with a fan.
Grandmother is filling the
brass altar cups with rice to
place on her altar. Spot on
Grandfather and Chieko.)*

Grandfather: Obon.
    Festival of the dead.
    The fires burn
    to guide us home.
    Ghosts are hungry
    journeying far.
    Sitting at the feast,
    they stir the brew of memory.

Jadine: Your sons. Ma. How is Hiro your legacy?

Michi: I keep losing everything.
    Have you seen the ladle with
    dented handle?
    My lacquer bowl?
    My pale green china vase.
    Everything just disappears.

Jadine: What happened to Hiro?

Michi: My red silk scarf.
    The flowers I cut this morning.
    Have you seen them?

Jadine: Ma. Why don't you ever talk about
    the camps?

Michi: Lost. The sugar cannister.
    The cast iron pan.
    Where are the teacups with blue leaves?
    See the orchard? Apples used to be
    bigger than his fists.
    All shriveled and sour.

Grandmother: We carried so many dreams with us.
    Over the ocean. The canefields.
    You cannot imagine the work.
    Before dawn would light our way,
    we were awake, boiling water,
    cooking.
    And then out into the sugar cane

	that ripped open our hands
	and broke his back.
Michi:	More work when we arrived here.
	But we were just getting somewhere.
	Then Mrs. H's husband disappeared.
	She thought he was dead in a ditch.
	Hit by a car. Shot by a thief.
	Huh. He was detained by the military.
	She didn't see him until after the war.
Grandmother:	We could have been bitter.
	Our mouths wrinkled and spitting up
	sighs of defeat.
Jadine:	I want to know about the camps.
Michi:	The camps?
	Just before the war, you were born. I thought it might be better to go see one of those women who do their business in the dark, plucking babies out of wombs with tweezers and coat hangers and hot wire sterilized by candlefire. We were so poor. Anything not to bring another mouth into the world.
	Fan the sushi rice.
Jadine:	I'm fanning.
Michi:	But I had you anyway. Fan!
Jadine:	I'm fanning.
Grandmother:	You were a beautiful baby girl.
Michi:	What calamity. I thought my
	mother-in-law would die.
	Keep fanning. *(voice angry)*
Jadine:	I'm fanning.
Michi:	A girl. Your father was so disappointed.
	Thank god Hiro and Russell came along.
	What would he have done if I didn't give
	him sons.
Grandmother:	You were a happy baby.
Michi:	Why, I'll never know. Well, what do you
	know but they bombed Pearl Harbor.
Jadine:	And we were sent to camp.

Michi:	We knew we were really in trouble. Keep fanning. Faster! *(voice angrier)*
Jadine:	I'm fanning. I'm fanning.
Michi:	My mother-in-law hated me. Said I was stuck up. I think she was jealous because I didn't look so Japanese. I tried to make her accept me. One day she shaved your head.
Grandmother:	You had such beautiful thick curly hair.
Michi:	Not like most nihonjin babies with straight ugly pricks of hair. She was jealous. Well that just got to me and I ran to my barrack and cried all day. Keep fanning. Faster.
Jadine:	*(softly)* The camps?
Grandmother:	*(Takes the sushi rice to the altar)* Namu amida butsu. Namu amida butsu. *(Dark except on Grandfather and Michi who walks into a single spot. She seems lost in memory, speaking to no one directly.)*
Grandfather:	It happened this way.
Michi:	We had gotten adjusted the best we could in those hot barracks. I was miserable. Big and pregnant again. My father was agitated because of our terrible diet. He'd roam around in the dust, kicking it in the air. I was so worried about him.
Grandfather:	Mushitte wa Mushitte wa gathering, gathering dust like memory swirling it in the wind.
Michi:	Papa was really angry this time. I felt responsible. He asked the camp authorities to give me some food with protein.
Grandfather:	Silence is a form of strength. More is said

	with wordless defiance.
Michi:	Papa was furious. They refused him. He's so proud. Hated to ask in the first place. He picked up a handful of sand and threw it toward the fence. The guard picks up his rifle.
Grandfather:	If we bend to foreign ways we do so as a matter of practicality. This is how we survive.
Michi:	I try to calm Papa. He's working himself into a rage. I'm really afraid. Days of nothing but rice and rutabaga. Rumor was the camp authorities had secreted a load of fowl. It seemed they deliberately wanted to starve us. The tower guard is smiling, aiming his rifle. I'm screaming at Papa. PAPA! He's running toward the guard, fists full of sand. I am sure I will hear the deafening crack. I can feel the bullet tear through my back. I can see Papa's body shattered, bloodied. My mouth opens. No sound comes out.
Grandfather:	We are here to be tested. We earn humanity with each burden we endure.
Michi:	Papa turns and throws the fistful of sand toward the tower and raises his shaking fist. I am sure I will see the bullet go through his heart and mine as I rush toward his side. I look for wounds. He is shaking in rage. I look up at the tower guard. He is laughing.
Grandfather:	Pine in winter. Bamboo in storm. We do not wither or break.

(Dim spot on Hiro at his window. We still cannot clearly see his size.)

Hiro: The spider is spinning very fast.
Web is repaired.
prepared for next victim.
I will capture flies.

> *(Dark on Hiro. Chieko walks
> into spot, unwrapping her
> obi, folding it carefully. Her
> kimono is loose, revealing
> contemporary dress.)*

Chieko: Threads of ourselves,
tied to history. Our journeys.
Body of my father, an abandoned farm.
Face of my mother, paper thin.
White voices like the tip of bayonets.
Barbed wire wraps us in time,
wraps us as a shroud.

> *(Chieko remains in spot.
> Lights up on the three women
> near the dining table.)*

Grandmother: Namu amida butsu.
Play music. Chieko's songs.

Jadine: Auntie Chieko who died so young?

Michi: She ruined herself. Madness. Cigarettes.
Starvation.

Jadine: Not normal.

Grandmother: She had a dream.

Michi: She wasted all your money for a stupid
dream. None of us can make it in their
world.

Jadine: The camps.

Grandmother: She wanted to be a star.

Jadine: Racism.

Michi: Will you shut up, Jadine! Chieko was
foolish. She wasted herself.

Grandmother: Grandfather loved her. He wanted only
to hear her sing.

Michi: And neglected the rest of us. We who
worked so hard for you to send *her* to
New York.

Grandmother:	She was beautiful. So talented.
Michi:	So mad.
Grandmother:	Please wind up the phonograph.
	For Bon.

> *(Jadine winds the old-fashioned phonograph, Grandmother's treasured antique. As the music plays, the lights dim on the three women. The music is Puccini's "Madame Butterfly", Cio Cio's aria, "One Fine Day". Spot is solely on Chieko. She pulls a bag close to her, packs the obi, pulls clothing out, drops them on the floor, packs them again. Speaks directly to audience.)*

Chieko: I am Cio Cio san.

Miss Nakano to you.

Excuse me, but I must begin my make up now. Hold all my calls, except for Joe, of course.

> *(Chieko starts to put on her make up, painting eyeliner, lipstick as she practices her scales.)*

La la la la la la

Ahhhh ahhhhh *(melody line from aria)*

No. They can't turn me down this time.

> *(Chieko holds various pieces of clothing from her bag up to her body, discards them, puts them back in her bag.)*

Joe served in the Army. Was sent to occupied Japan. He says the most beautiful women in the world are from the Orient. He was tempted to bring one home. But was glad he didn't because he met me.

Right here in New York.

If father knew, he'd have a fit, me dating a hakujin. Ahhhh ahhhhh *(continues melody line)* Oh, you Sansei. You have it easy now. You can marry anyone you want. They even have movies and plays with all oriental casts. Imagine that! When I started out, I was the only one trying to make it in the opera world. They tried to discourage me.

Huh. Miss Nakano to you.

But I don't give up easily.

They wouldn't let me stay in certain places...so many people still hated the *Japs* they'd call me.

Miss Nakano to you.

Have I received any phone calls?

Joe says we really know how to take care of our men. When we met, he asked me out to dinner. *(whispers)* I was starving, being on such a strict budget.

We went to this little Italian restaurant where they played opera music. It was so romantic.

> *(Chieko sings another line*
> *from Butterfly's love song.*
> *She dances in her spotlight*
> *with her hands clasped.)*

Well, confidentially, we went to a hotel. I was so embarrassed. He told the clerk I was his warbride. Joe believed in me. Encouraged me. Said I'd be the first Nisei opera star in America.

> *(Chieko sings a little more*
> *fiercely. Her voice begins*
> *to crack slightly)*

At my audition they kept mispronouncing my name.

Nakamuu, Nakaow, Nakenoo. Huh.

I just sang my heart out anyway.
Joe made me feel beautiful, like a star.
I loved to please him.
I'd massage his back for hours.

*(Chieko pulls the obi from
her bag, caresses it as she
slowly unfolds it.)*

You liberated Sansei women might laugh
but let me tell you, a man wants to be
treated like a king.

*(Chieko sings again, her
voice sounding slighty
more strained.)*

Yes, we've paved some roads for you,
and our feet have bled. I'll tell you, it
hasn't been easy.

*(Chieko's voice changes to a
nasal, flat, voice unlike her
own.)*

Miss. O Miss. You're not scheduled to audi-
tion. The cast has been selected. Don't re-
call any, uh, orientals in this production.
Please. Off the stage.

*(Chieko responds to the
voice she has created, turns
to stage right.)*

Miss Nakano to you.

*(Chieko sings another line
from Butterfly's song, her
voice showing much more
intensity.)*

I'm expecting a very important
phone call.
Joe and I would have to be careful where
we went together. There was so much
prejudice...

*(Chieko's voice changes
again to hostile, flat twang.)*

Hey. Lady. You'll have to clear the stage.

*(Chieko shakes the obi she is
holding toward the created
voice, stage right.)*

N A K A N O ! You won't forget it
when it's in lights. Father will be proud.
He's sacrificed so much for me.
And you. Sansei. It's not easy.
Where's my purse? *(searching, snatching
it up frantically)* They're always trying to
steal something from you.

*(Chieko pulls out a handker-
chief from her purse)*

Joe gave me this handkerchief. With lace
on the borders. Had to use it to stop the
bleeding after my uh, umm operation.

*(Chieko's voice changes to
one of rage, impatience,
shouting)*

Hey you! Get off the stage!!!

*(Chieko is now grotesque.
Her kimono disheveled, her
makeup running, clownish,
a parody of exaggerated
"orientalized" features with
black eyeliner curving her
eyes to her temples. She
sings a line from the suicide
aria, and her voice chokes
on the high notes. She throws
the obi across the stage.)*

MISS NAKANO TO YOU!!!
(more softly) Are you ready for my solo?
I don't have all day. I'm expecting a very
important phone call.

*(Chieko's head is high. She
is posed as a true opera star,
almost haughty in her
pride.)*

See, Sansei? It isn't easy.

(Lights up on Grandfather. As he speaks, Chieko walks to him, hands him the end of her unfurled obi. She as if in a ritual, dresses in her kimono, wrapping the obi neatly, as he holds it taut.)

Grandfather: Bon.
Fires flicker, lighting the way
for the dead, returning home.
The dead circle, seeking
solace.
Embers of dreams unfulfilled,
one by one,
each gathering,
each expire in me.

(Lights up on Michi and Jadine at dining table.)

Jadine: I never want to get married.

Michi: With your mouth, you won't have to worry about it.

Jadine: Relationships, Ma. That means relating... to each other.

Michi: A man is security. Without a husband, you shrivel up like a sour plum. No grandchildren. An infertile desert.

Jadine: Times are changing. Marriage is outdated.

Michi: Everyone must have a family. When the world spits on you, you can turn to your family.

Jadine: *(aside)* Even they will reject you.

Michi: Only your family really cares.

Jadine: *(aside)* Except for the ones in the litter who are unacceptable, who hold up mirrors of someone you don't want to see.

Michi: There is nothing like the joy of your children... watching them grow, fulfilling their needs...

Jadine: *(aside)* Some are sacrificed... for the

favor of others. Aren't females always sacrificed for the well-being of the tribe?

Michi: Good children will take care of you in your old age.

Jadine: Children grow up and leave...the ones who survive.

Michi: Not if they've been raised properly. My children are mine forever.

Jadine: It is no wonder we are lonely.

Michi: Do you know about loneliness?

The feel of empty rooms, swallowing you? No warmth. No sound. No comfort? You do not know if you exist.

So you talk to the mirrors. The wall. The sink.

Jadine: Being ignored or locked up.

Being expendable.

Michi: We'll do anything to escape loneliness.

Jadine: Search for mothers and fathers and brothers who will accept you?

Michi: A family...

Jadine: What about love?

Michi: Love matters less as you grow old.

Jadine: I'm getting very depressed.

Michi: You find someone who it seems will fill your life like that piece of sky that fits perfectly over the trees in your field. Sleeves for your bare branches. A garment in winter. We'll do anything to get that. So when the years shrivel and children grow and war and distances and work wears the sleeves of love, lonely is patches on sheets washed thin, a sleepless night sky. Lonely is when he doesn't feel when he touches or talk when he speaks, when words are too familiar like "rice", "tea" or "too tired." But you remember the terror of talking to the sink, so you put up with the less empty

	pain of complaints about cold food and sick chickens and backaches. Your comfort is knowing your bed is not empty.
Jadine:	I want more than that.
Michi:	First get a man.
Jadine:	Ma! I don't want what you got.
Michi:	WHAT WILL PEOPLE THINK???
Jadine:	That I'm not respectable.
Michi:	I'm your mother. I want you to have security. Why did we spend all that money on your education?
Jadine:	So I could find a good husband?
Michi:	You're getting too old to catch a man.
Jadine:	*Catch* a man...
	(Lights up on Russell, Haru, Tosh. They are standing stage opposite from the women, facing each other.)
Russell:	Independent women.
Haru:	Smart mouth. See what it gets her.
Tosh:	All the answers and an empty bed.
Michi:	Die an old maid.
Jadine:	Hey, ma. I've tried. The lawyer who graduated from Yale.
Michi:	He was from a good family.
Jadine:	He kept combing his hair.
Russell:	Listen to his every word. Pretend he's brilliant.
Haru:	Wear white.
Tosh:	Don't let him in your pants until after two dinners.
Michi:	He would want a good wife.
Jadine:	No, dessert.
Michi:	Lots of nice men out there.
Jadine:	The intern who talked about his sports car.
Russell:	Choose your words. Seem vulnerable. Smile a lot. Cling.
Haru:	Keep the knees locked together.

Tosh:	Don't open them until the war is over.
Jadine:	The engineer from U.C.
Michi:	Invite him to dinner.
Jadine:	I hate silent movies.
Russell:	Make him think he's the center of the world. Be obedient, trustworthy, faithful.
Haru:	Wear the dress with buttons that lock.
Tosh:	No one wants damaged goods.

*(Lights dark on the men.
Stage dims, spot on Jadine.)*

Jadine: The sound of shakuhachi
is oozing around my mind.

*(Traditional shakuhachi or
flute music plays softly in
background.)*

Beautiful samurai warrior
squared in the snow,
with eye-blinking speed
sliced the wind
and his opponent,
blood bursting the cold air.
His woman is looking on
in the high field,
breasts heaving,
obi flying.
He squares his back,
sheathes his sword, locks his hands,
shoulders keeping time
to his leaving her behind.
Toshiro.
You don't ever get down
with your women.
Why don't you?
I can really get into you
sitting in that meditation room alone,
sifting the thoughts of your ancestors,
mind and body
one with your sword.
But.

Must you scorn her all the time?
Don't misunderstand...
I really dig
that ritual,
that clear, clean blade
of discipline,
that taut wire
connected to the Way of the Warrior.
Your gathering all time
into moment beyond all time,
that put/feeling/aside
oneness with nature/self
perfectly in tune
      like the
          "bell ringing in an
          empty sky"
      like the
          flute crying alone
      like the
          sound of sun on
          stone.
And oh, Mifune.
You are so fine
I can sit with you for hours
and wait
and wait
for that climax,
for that instant whipping of your blade
          chhhhhaaaaaap!!!
but as you walk off
in the wind blown lonely
twilight,
without even looking back,
your high, wide
stepping in time
to Japanese cowboy music,
I am that woman
kimono clad,
silent and motionless

(except for heaving breast)
suppressing all the frustration/emptiness
not wanting that loneliness

I am that hair
tearing, hara-kiri prone,
longing/licking
body-burning-for-you
woman of the dunes.

Turn around, Mifune!!
Stop cleaning your blade.
    We can make
    an eternity
    together.
        (Dark on Jadine. Lights
        gradually up on Michi.
        Jadine enters light.)

Michi:	You better think about the future, starting your own family before it's too late.
Jadine:	I've got my work.
Michi:	You call that work? All that political stuff. Where's it going to get you? Who cares about what happened over thirty-five years ago? Ancient history. And what you call it? Civil rights cases? We've come a long ways. Don't make trouble for yourself.
Jadine:	There's trouble, Ma, anyway. We haven't come that far. Don't fool yourself. Who's still at the bottom of the American heap? We just climb over each other...
Michi:	Enough! No one cares if you're poor and old. You'll never catch a man with your mouth...
Jadine:	My mouth! It betrays me. It has it's own life.

I paint it, set it in a smile.
Clamp both hands over it.
Pinch the lips together.
My tongue climbs out between
my fingers.
Pounces on the poor man.
He sees how grotesque it is.
It takes him by surprise.
I try to retrieve it, put it in its place.
It escapes again.

Michi: Don't be sarcastic with me.

Jadine: Never, Ma. It's like having warts. You don't choose to have them...thoughts just popping out.

Michi: I've struggled by myself too, Jadine. It was frightening. I thought I would die and no one would know...

Jadine: There are different kinds of death. I have to choose my own.

Michi: You're on dangerous ground.

Jadine: Life's dangerous, Ma.

> *(Lights dim. Spot on Chieko. She dances with obi in her hands while she tells a parable.)*

Chieko: The youngest daughter of a poor farmer was sold to a wealthy old man. The old man was afraid the girl would run away so he tied her waist with a rope, the other end tied to his wrist. Even when he slept, he kept the rope taut between them. He treated her kindly, but would not release the rope, tugging it constantly to reassure himself that she was present. When the old man died, his son inherited his house and the servant girl. The son prided himself in being more modern and liberal than his father, kept the rope tied to the young servant girl's waist, but lengthened it so that she would have more freedom of movement. She was even able to wander far into the fields and riverbanks by herself. But the young servant girl, without the constant tautness between her and her master, mourned deeply. The son, who could not understand her sorrow, loosened the rope more and more. Finally, the girl threw herself in the river and drowned, miles of loose rope floating above her.

> *(Lights up on Tosh and Russell. As they speak, Chieko in dim light floats to Grandfather, hands him the end of the obi and repeats the ritual of wrapping.)*

Tosh: Between the nunnery and nymphomania...

Russell: We try to keep them trembling...

Tosh: To hide, conceal that we are afraid.

Russell: We can't let it go,
the wire we hold taut...

Tosh: On which they walk, balanced...

Russell: Or ever reveal our fear...

Tosh: Never.
(Walks downstage to spot) I wake up in the middle of the night. Sweating. My mouth is wide open. But there is no noise. No breath. It's like I am drowning.

Russell: Drowning... *(joining Tosh downstage)*

Tosh: The scream is underwater. Only silent bubbles stream from my mouth. My lungs are bursting.

Russell: But don't let on.
Don't feel.
Sometimes when I was a little boy, I'd call out for my father in the night. Scared, imagining shadows moving in the dark.
And SHE would come.
Whisper to me not to wake him up. If he hears, he'll tell me to act like a man.

Tosh: Water filling my lungs
my hands clutching at anything

	to pull myself up. Nothing but water. Water.
Russell:	Eyes like steel. He couldn't stand to see me cry. Even when I was five years old. Damn. Called me ona...woman...
Tosh:	They called me Jap.
Russell:	Ona. Only woman is afraid.
Tosh:	*(whispering)* Jap. There's one of you!! *(Jumping up to foot of stage)* Goddamn yellow sonofabitch. Sneaky motherfucker. Nah. Not one of my relatives. I'm an American.
Russell:	And I couldn't fight back.
Tosh:	Couldn't fight back.
Russell:	*(now also at foot of stage, hand to forehead, saluting audience)* "You are not being accused of any crime..."
Tosh:	They first put me in mess. I cooked for them. They wanted me to taste the food first. Afraid I'd poison them. I was their "translator" when they'd break radio code. But they made me cook for them.
Russell:	"You should be glad to make the sacrifice to prove your loyalty..."
Tosh:	When I refused to taste the food, they jammed it in my mouth, pushed my head back like a chicken's.
Russell:	"It's your contribution to the war effort..."
Tosh:	And they'd laugh. While I choked and they shoved more food in my mouth. I flopped like a fish, vomiting.
Russell:	"There may be one of you who threatens our national security..."
Tosh:	I told them to kill me outright. Throw me in the ocean so I could float back home to ports of California. Beach myself like a whale. Let

	the gulls eat my heart.
Russell:	*(pointing to the audience)* One among you is dangerous.
Tosh:	But they just laughed.
Russell:	*(still pointing)* You are dangerous.
	(Dark on Russell and Tosh. Spot on Grandfather and Chieko. Lights dimly on Haru and Michi at dining table.)
Grandfather:	Bonsai, twisted bent, shaped by the wind. These trees made stronger by adversity.
Chieko:	Why does the slavegirl not cut the rope? Untie herself? Why does it take you so long to ask? Cut the rope!
Haru:	Hey, Michi. The baby's crying.
Michi:	No, I just looked in on him. He's fine. Playing quietly.
Haru:	He's a good son. Going to be somebody.
Michi:	Maybe he should stay here on the farm with us. You're not getting any younger, Haru.
Haru:	No, he's not going to be a farmer. Get his hands dirty. Too hard this work. Better for him to go to college.
Michi:	And he'll buy all the things we can't afford now. A new kitchen. Hiro will get me a stainless steel sink with a garbage disposal.
Haru:	We'll go fishing together in a boat with a motor. China Lake. A strong boat. So I won't worry about drifting out too far.
Michi:	And silk dresses. Like Clara's that float in the breeze.
	(Tosh enters. They stop talking instantly.)
Tosh:	You fantasizing about Hiro again? How he's gonna win the Nobel Peace Prize?

Haru: When are you leaving? You've outstayed your welcome.

Tosh: That's the trouble when you're trying to hide. We keep finding you.

Haru: Good for nothing. A drunk! I don't know how we've put up with you this long.

Michi: Please. You'll disturb Hiro.

Tosh: Disturb Hiro? I'm not in your fantasyland. You can't disturb Hiro.

Haru: Shut up! Drunkard.

Tosh: Bon. Festival of the dead. You buried the past.

Haru: Get out.

Tosh: Kind sister. I will leave. But your suffering. End your suffering. Take Hiro to get help.

Michi: *(Is crying)*

Haru: *(Furious)* Don't talk like that in this house. Your damn mouth. What it get you? Your wife left you. Ha. Probably for another man. Don't blame her.

> *(Michi moves to step between Tosh and Haru. Tosh is angry, stumbling, swaying, swinging his fists at Haru. Haru grabs his shirt. Russell, Jadine, Grandmother rush in. Pulling them apart. Music from offstage plays softly. A traditional Japanese lullaby. All freeze.)*

Grandmother: Namu amida butsu.

> *(Everyone is still and watches as Hiro, a grown man, chases his rubber ball. He jumps, claps in child-like movements as he catches it, drops it, laughing as a child. He drops the ball and chases it off stage. Lights dim.)*

Grandmother:	Namu amida butsu.
Chieko:	Rope, wire, threads of silk, umbilical cords tied to our hearts. The past is bound gagged, stifled, smothered. Air cut off. Corridors cobwebbed lead to endless deserts. Swamps that lay like a trap. Spider's silk like barbed wire awaiting lunch. Cut the rope.

> *(Slide on backdrop of rows of barracks. Stage is dark except for Michi lying on a cot spotted in a barren room. She is obviously in pain of labor. Grandmother and Haru are present with her.)*

Grandmother:	They won't come?
Haru:	The nurse at the infirmary said, "babies are born every minute."
Grandmother:	Heartless as these barren deserts.
Haru:	They're busy. We have to wait they said.
Grandmother:	This is not good. Birth delayed too long. The baby will not turn without help. Michi is losing strength.
Haru:	*(pacing)* We'll name him Hiromi. "Beautiful abundance".
Grandmother:	I'm afraid for this child.
Haru:	We'll call him Hiro. Strong boy.

> *(Slide fades, stage dark.*
> *Lights up on present family.)*

Grandmother:	Namu amida butsu.
Tosh:	Yea, the casualties were very high.
Haru:	Please. Get out.
Grandmother:	We brought so much with us. Dreams. Children.

Dreams for Grandchildren.
Gave up everything.
Picked up. Moved on.
Built again.

(Slides of train carload of people. It is the past. Relocation trains. Jadine and Russell walk into the slide, juxtaposing past and present.)

Jadine: It's funny. When everyone is suffering...

Russell: We help each other...

Grandmother: We were all in shock. Five days to sell everything. Pack what we could carry. No one knew what to expect. Your mother was pregnant. Sick. Strangers were compassionate. Shared their water. An old woman rubbed your mother's aching back. We did not know who she was and your mother wept at her kindness.

Russell: I guess we see ourselves in these times. At first, I was really mad that we didn't fight back.

Jadine: Really mad.

Russell: What would we have done?

Jadine: Same thing, back then.

Russell: So who are you mad at now, Jadine? The world?

Jadine: Born in America. Can't ignore the wounds.

(Slide fades. Lights up on present family.)

Not even you, bro.

Russell: Your crusading's like a corset. Shit. You're cold.

Jadine: My anger is comfortable to me. Makes me think I'll survive.

Russell: Survive what? You got out alive. What've you got to fight?

Jadine: Not you, I hope.

Russell: You think you're oppressed. By everybody.

Jadine:	No. I know *their* indifference like the feel of shiver on my skin. Their eyes are glassy, opaque. Blind to me. I vanish before them like water in the desert. But to you, I am unacceptable.
Russell:	Power structures don't give a shit about your search for significance. Me…you make me feel uncomfortable.
Jadine:	Russ, I don't want to push you away. I don't want to be a victim to society either. My anger's become comfortable. It's how I measure myself.
Russell:	Society measures us in terms of power. Power is my Porsche, my credit rating, the girl on my arm. My house, my paintings, my ability to buy visibility.
Jadine:	A comfortable existence.
Russell:	It's my choice. You make me squirm when you're my mirror, sis. Because then, I feel as invisible as you.
Jadine:	Who did the job on us? Those who orchestrate suffering.
Russell:	Those who we have to prove ourselves to.
Jadine:	No, that's you, bro.
Russell:	Then who do we have? Where do we go?
Jadine:	To the ones who share the suffering.
Tosh:	Hey! You two. It's party time.
Jadine:	Gotta open up the wounds. Let them breathe. This family's festering.
Russell:	Give it a rest, Jay.
Tosh:	Personally, I think open wounds should be treated with alcohol, right Doc?
Russell:	Not total submersion, unc. You'll drown.
Tosh:	Funny guy.

(Spot on Grandfather and Chieko.)

Grandfather:	Memory is the stick that is used to beat you. Keep you alert. Watch your back.

Chieko:	Miles of cord
	floating above you.
	Cut the rope.
Jadine:	Secrets.
Russell:	Say something.
Tosh:	Terrible.
Russell:	The void.
Jadine:	I want to know. It's my story, too.
Russell:	Dark rooms. Shadows moving.
Jadine:	Not normal.
	My mother's shame.
	Deep, scathing...
Michi:	His life, hidden in dark corners whispered
	in cobwebs...
Grandmother:	Truth, boiling like light, no doctors,
	no boiling water...
Haru:	In camp we were not trusted
	with cooking fire...
Grandmother:	The child came out, pushing with
	terrible rage
	against being enclosed, encaged...
Michi:	Pushed back in...
Grandmother:	Mada, Mada
	sono toi denai
Michi:	It isn't time.
	It isn't time.
Haru:	He broke the chain, the cord,
	smothered in his mother's cage,
	smothered his brain...
Grandmother:	He, we
	came out again...
Jadine:	Not normal.
Tosh:	The taint
	not in his brain.
Grandmother:	To uso
	To haji
	fukaku chi no naka ni...

Russell:	The lies, the shame, blood deep.
Tosh:	Japanese in prison camps…
Jadine:	Not normal at all.
Tosh:	Came back from the army, a war hero. Showed my loyalty. Proved I was a man. They couldn't break me. I thought about my wife a lot. Helped get me through the rough times. She was pregnant. Insisted it was mine. <div style="text-align:center">*(Tosh counts on his fingers to twelve)*</div>I couldn't sleep after that.
Jadine:	We can't count the losses.
Russell:	Can't bring back the losses.
Michi:	Remember what's important now.
Haru:	What's important…
Hiro:	*(Enters weeping)* Spider's gone.
Russell:	Gone to lay her eggs.
Michi:	She'll be back.
Hiro:	I wait by the window where she spins across the sky, she ties thread to my waist and tells me to hide. The wind whirls me up over fields where lilies grow, over the riverbanks where water curls like rope. Wait by the window and she'll spin across the sky, Dew rests on her threads like tears in my eye…
Chieko:	Silk thread spun. Wrapped in obi, rope, cord.

These bodies
a tight winter cocoon.
Spring comes like a hand
untying knots,
slowly, we unwrap, emerge.
Reveal ourselves.

Grandmother: We didn't complain.
Injustices were great.
Didn't throw up our hands
and relent to despair,
choke on strings of sorrow.
We did not make ourselves extinct.
We stayed. Rightfully our place.
Namu amida butsu.

Michi: Thirty-eight years of not talking about it.
Keeping quiet. I can't forget it. Don't
want to. What they did to my son. Can't
change it, but don't want them to forget
it either.

Haru: The smell was terrible in those stalls.
We did the best we could. Dug around
and pulled up manure. Treated worse
than animals. Your mother kept us
together. She had guts. Wrote to au-
thorities. Had guts.

Jadine: Reparations. No more camps.
Russell: Dangerous shit, man. Sitting on the side-
lines. Keeping quiet. Can't be quiet no
more.

Tosh: Shit no.
Hiro: Spiders are weaving stories.

> *(Chieko floats into spot.*
> *She is beautiful once more.*
> *Neatly combed as before,*
> *completely dressed in white*
> *kimono and tied obi.)*

Chieko: One end of obi
held in his hands.
The other end,
I will wrap into thin red stem,

my face the blossom.
I tell you the story,
loosening knots, unraveling tangles.
Various ends of string floating
in the wind.
I unravel, cut,
bind, unwrap.
Forever finding
another loose end.
But I can sing.
As I constantly pull,
constantly mend,
I sing.
I tell you, Sansei.
It isn't easy.

Grandfather: Webs of memory.
                Songs.
                Stories that scream from our
                hearts split in two.
                Bon. Festival of the dead.
                I travel in the smoking embers,
                Chieko's songs
                shaped from desert flowers, shell,
                stone.
                Sand gardens swirling into eternity.

Russell: We are strange.
            Haru would make me wake up at five in
            the morning to go gardening with him.
            Because he wanted me to become a sur-
            geon. Suffer from the bottom and look
            up. Never forget the bottom.
            The suffering.
            Japanese are funny that way.

Jadine: Ma would re-wrap my Christmas presents
           and give them to someone else. She said
           she couldn't stand the humiliation of get-
           ting and not giving.
           Japanese are funny that way.

Tosh: There are things we want to forget but

we can't. So we pretend for a long time
they didn't happen.
Japanese are funny, *(laughs)*
Don't want to make anybody
uncomfortable.

Grandmother: Plant the seeds.
Grow the crops.
Harvest its yield, Sansei.
Justice will be done.

Michi: Hiro is sleeping.

> *(sings traditional Japanese*
> *lullaby)*
> Nennen kororiyo
>   Okoro riyo.

Sleep little child
though there's trouble at the gate.
Your father's in potato fields
and won't be home till late.
When the gate is opened, we will again
be free.
This land is yours and mine as far as we
can see.

Haru: At the window, he plays,
cobwebs he won't let me sweep away,
watching spiders spinning all day.

Tosh: Hiro is timeless, like the moon.

Grandmother: Namu amida butsu.

Jadine Bon. Festival of the dead.
Come home.
Unbury the past. Lay it to rest.
Work to be done tomorrow.

Russell: Give it a rest, Jay. Your mouth.

Jadine: Watch out, bro. She's after you.

Russell: I can count on it.

Tosh: Let's all have a drink.

> *(They gather at the table to*
> *toast and feast. Grand-*
> *father and Chieko float*
> *off stage, singing.)*

Grandfather: Moon is rising
over smoking coals of Bon fires.

Chieko: Soon the night will hear
the songs of lovers meeting.

Glossary

Concentration (Internment) Camps: Ten sites in which Japanese Americans were interned during World War II.

Manzanar, California
Tule Lake, California
Poston, Arizona
Gila River, Arizona
Minidoka, Idaho
Heart Mountain, Wyoming
Granada, Colorado
Topaz, Utah
Rohwer, Arkansas
Jerome, Arkansas

Total capacity of the ten camps: 120,000 people. Each site was isolated in deserts or swampy delta areas, with severe weather conditions, undeveloped land and soil unsuitable for cultivation.

"The mosquitos at Rohwer were the worst. Bigger than your baby fist. They'd get through our nets and we could hear them buzzsawing in our ear...you were one big mosquito welt. Yea, they loved your soft baby skin for dessert..." *(My cousin, John)*

Issei: Generation of Japanese who emigrated to the United States, referred to as the First Generation.

Nisei: First generation of Japanese Americans born in the United States, but referred to as the Second Generation.

Sansei: Third Generation Japanese Americans.

Yonsei: Fourth Generation Japanese Americans.

Bon Festival: In Japan, *Bon* is observed in mid-August to commemorate the spirits of the dead. It is also called the Festival of Lanterns (fires and lanterns are lit to guide the souls to their homes).

Many Japanese American communities celebrate *Bon* during the summer months with songs and dances passed from generation to generation. Originally a somber and melancholy Buddhist ceremony with chants, prayers and dance in a mass for the spirits of the dead, in contemporary times *Bon* has become an occasion for festivity and celebration, the coming together of families and community.

"Tsuki ga deta deta...": Lyrics from "Tanko Bushi" or "The Coal Miner's Song from Kyushu", a folk song and dance popular also in the Japanese American communities for its simplicity of movements which depict the work of coalminers digging for coal and pushing their carts. Sung and danced by celebrants at festivals and banquets.

"Shina no yoru...": Lyrics from "China Nights" a song popular in the Japanese American communities during the 40's and 50's. Many Nisei heard and learned the song for the first time while interned in the camps. It is said that the Kibei (born in the U.S. but educated in Japan) popularized the song

from Japan in America. "China Nights" is a melancholy and nostalgic love song recalling the past.

Namu Amida Butsu: A Buddhist prayer/chant. Recitation is an act of reverence to the glory of Amida Buddha.

Shakuhachi: Bamboo flute which has a breathy, haunting quality of sound.

Obi: A long, wide, heavy decorative sash tightly encircled several times completing the kimono outfit. It is bound from the bosom to the waist and tied at the back to display the design of the loop and woven tapestry of the obi.

The obi compels a straight spine posture.

"I hate wearing the damn thing. You can't even take a deep breath let alone sing! I think the obi was invented by men to confine our steps and constrict our voices..." *(Aunt Chiyo)*